W0052065

Pulse

WORKBOOK

von
Elizabeth Hine
Angela Lloyd
William McNeice
Ingrid Preedy
Isobel Williams
Steve Williams

unter Mitarbeit der Verlagsredaktion

Cornelsen

Liebe Lernende,

das **Pulse Workbook** ist mehr als ein Arbeitsheft – durch die *PagePlayer*-App wird es für Sie zum Sprungbrett in die digitale Welt.

Am Puls der Technik – mit der *PagePlayer*-App

Die *PagePlayer*-App bietet Ihnen die Möglichkeit, mit Ihrem Smartphone oder Tablet auf alle digitalen Inhalte des Arbeitsheftes (Audio- und Video-Dateien) zuzugreifen – ganz ohne CD oder DVD! Schnell, intuitiv und komfortabel – der *PagePlayer* ist die flexible und zeitgemäße Art, das Hör- und Sehverstehen auch unterwegs zu trainieren.

Und so geht es:
1. Laden Sie den kostenlosen *PagePlayer* im App Store Ihres Smartphones oder Tablets (oder auf www.cornelsen.de/pageplayer) herunter.
2. Öffnen Sie den *PagePlayer* und laden Sie dort kapitelweise die Inhalte zum **Pulse Workbook** herunter.
3. Halten Sie Ihr Smartphone oder Tablet über die Buchseite. Sogleich werden Ihnen alle abspielbereiten Hörtexte und Videoclips in einem Medienmenü angezeigt.
4. Wählen Sie das gewünschte Element aus, drücken Sie *Play* – und los geht's

Alternativ können Sie die Medien für die Nutzung ohne mobiles Gerät unter www.cornelsen.de/webcodes mit dem folgenden Webcode aufrufen:

▶ PULSE-WB-MEDIA

Wir hoffen, dass Ihnen die Arbeit mit dem **Pulse Workbook** viel Spaß macht!

Die Autoren und der Verlag

TABLE OF CONTENTS

Exam skills and strategies

1 The road ahead

A A good first impression

1 Word power: different jobs and careers

A How many jobs and careers do you know? Complete the table by putting the jobs in the box into the correct category.

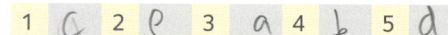

Sales Assistant • Copywriter • Photographer • Finance Manager • Accountant • Store Manager • Plumber • Film and Video Editor • Banker • Electrician • Hairdresser • Cashier

Marketing and advertising	Finance	Retail	Services
Copy writer ₁	Finance manager ₄	Sales assistant ₇	Plumber ₁₀
Film/video editor ₂	Banker ₅	Store Manager ₈	Hairdresser ₁₁
Photographer ₃	Accountant ₆	Cashier ₉	Electrician ₁₂

B Match the two parts to make collocations related to jobs and careers.

1 to apply for   a an interview
2 to work with   b travelling
3 to attend   c a job
4 to enjoy   d a language
5 to be fluent in   e people

1 C   2 e   3 a   4 b   5 d

2 Reading: a job advert

A Read the advert and highlight the adjectives the employer wants to see the candidate demonstrate.

Employer:	Simplicity
Posted:	12 April 20..
Ref:	SPSH379H
Contact:	Mark Snoek
Location:	Luxembourg
Function:	Intern
Hours:	Part-time

Apply with CV and covering letter

Web Developer Intern (m/f)   **SIMPLICITY**

Simplicity is a fast-growing startup that creates simplified tourist maps of cities, enabling tourists to navigate their way through an unfamiliar city with ease.

We are looking for bright, intelligent and hard-working interns to carry out essential day-to-day tasks in our Luxembourg office.

The successful candidate will have either a university degree or be in the final year of the course. He or she should have some experience with Android and IOS programming, be independently-minded and should be able to work without supervision.

B When writing a covering letter, it is better to describe yourself by giving an example than by simply repeating the adjective used in the advert. Choose three adjectives and write sentences that illustrate your suitability for a job of your choice.

For example: hard-working   *While at school, I had also had a part-time job.*

3

Making changes: healthy eating

Put the words in the right order to make sentences.

1   any / Don't / meals / eat / between / snacks

_____

2   breakfast / to school / without / Don't / go / eating / any

_____

3   Some / salt / contain / ready meals / too much

_____

4   meal / water / Always / drink / your / some / with.

_____

5   My / ready meals / any / mother / buys / never

_____

6   always / vegetables / She / serves some / the meal / with

_____

4

3

Listening: an interview with a nutritionist

A   Listen to Fran's interview with Andrew Ferrie and answer the following questions.

1   Where is the interview taking place?
2   Why are different foodstuffs being chopped up?
3   Why does Fran prefer chicken burgers to beef burgers?
4   How much chicken meat is in a chicken burger?
5   What other natural ingredients go into a chicken burger?
6   What kind of burgers does Andrew eat and why?

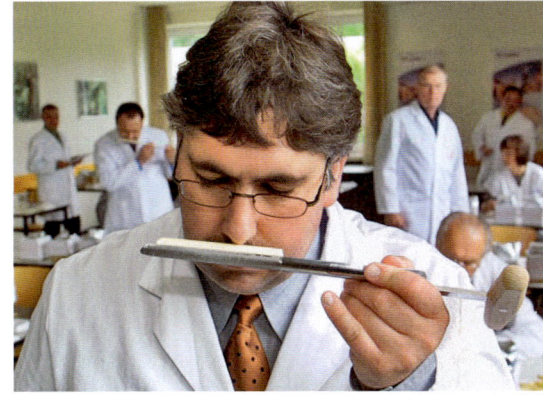

B   Read the following extracts from the interview and decide which words and phrases from the box can replace the highlighted expressions.

> animals • chemicals that are used to kill insects • completely artificial •
> food you can prepare quickly and easily • given food • least expensive parts of the animals •
> non-food substances • treated with medicine • what goes into the food

1   When we're talking about the food industry, a lot of these natural ingredients are mixed with other things which are not natural at all.

_____

2   There are industrial chemicals in every type of fast-food burger we've tested.

_____

3   The meat … comes from the cheapest parts of the carcasses.

_____

4   The livestock has been medicated with pharmaceuticals and fed products that are contaminated with pesticides.

_____

B The other end of the scale

1

Word power: talking about eating disorders

Match 1–10 with a–j to make sentences we can use to talk about eating disorders. The words and expressions on are all on page 24 of the Student's Book.

1 Anorexia is an emotional disorder	a a person's feelings of the (sexual) attractiveness of their own body.
2 The expression "body image" refers to	b the belief that extreme dieting is a good way to lose weight.
3 Bulimia is an emotional disorder	c a person who is so thin that you can see his/her bones.
4 Dieting is	d a person you admire and try to copy.
5 The expression "eating disorders" refers to the emotional disorders	e eating less food or food only of a particular type in order to lose weight.
6 The expression "frail physique" describes	f in which there is an abnormal fear of being fat, causing the person to stop eating and leading to dangerous weight loss.
7 The expression "pro-anorexia" describes	g in which a person repeatedly eats too much and then forces him/herself to be sick.
8 A role model is	h that cause eating habits that are not normal.
9 The adjective "skeletal" describes	i the body of a person who is physically weak and thin.
10 The adjective "skinny" is used in a disapproving way	j to describe someone whose thinness is unpleasant or makes them look ugly.

1	2	3	4	5	6	7	8	9	10

2

Reading: fashion models as role models

> Schwierige Texte lesen: SB p. 210

A Choose the better word or phrase from the brackets to complete the text. There is only one correct answer each time. Remember to read what comes before and after the words in brackets.

Choices – an extremely thin figure or a long, healthy life?

Isabelle Caro, who died in 2007 as a result of too much (pro-anorexia / dieting)[1] is not the only model who lost weight in order to keep her job as a top model. Even though many of them develop (eating disorders / dieting)[2], the fashion industry does not attempt to help the models to get over their serious illnesses, and designers continue to present their clothes on (skeletal / bulimia)[3] figures. The people in the business know that a thin body shows off the clothes well. Worrying about your (body image / role model)[4] is a part of growing up. Teenagers look up to people they see in the media and often copy the behaviour of the (role model / frail physique)[5] they adore. When they study the hair, make-up and (frail physiques / body image)[6] of the fashion models in magazines or TV, teenagers don't see people with (dieting / eating disorders)[7], they see rich and successful women with bodies they would like to have. Even though these (dieting / skinny)[8] women are ugly and unpleasant to look at, many teenagers view them as beautiful. Many of these teenagers will develop (anorexia / bulimia)[9] because they are afraid to get fat. In an attempt to keep their weight down, some will use (anorexia / bulimia)[10], alternately eating too much, then sticking their fingers down their throats in order to bring the food back up again.

Some models get treatment and recover from their illnesses but those who don't, die. Isabelle Caro was one of these models. When she died, many (pro-anorexia / dieting)[11] forums showed pictures of her and said she looked beautiful. As a doctor in the hospital where Isabelle Caro died said, "No one who has an (anorexia / eating disorder)[12] looks beautiful at any time."

B Some people were interviewed on their views on eating disorders. Match what they said to the speakers below. There is one speaker more than you need.

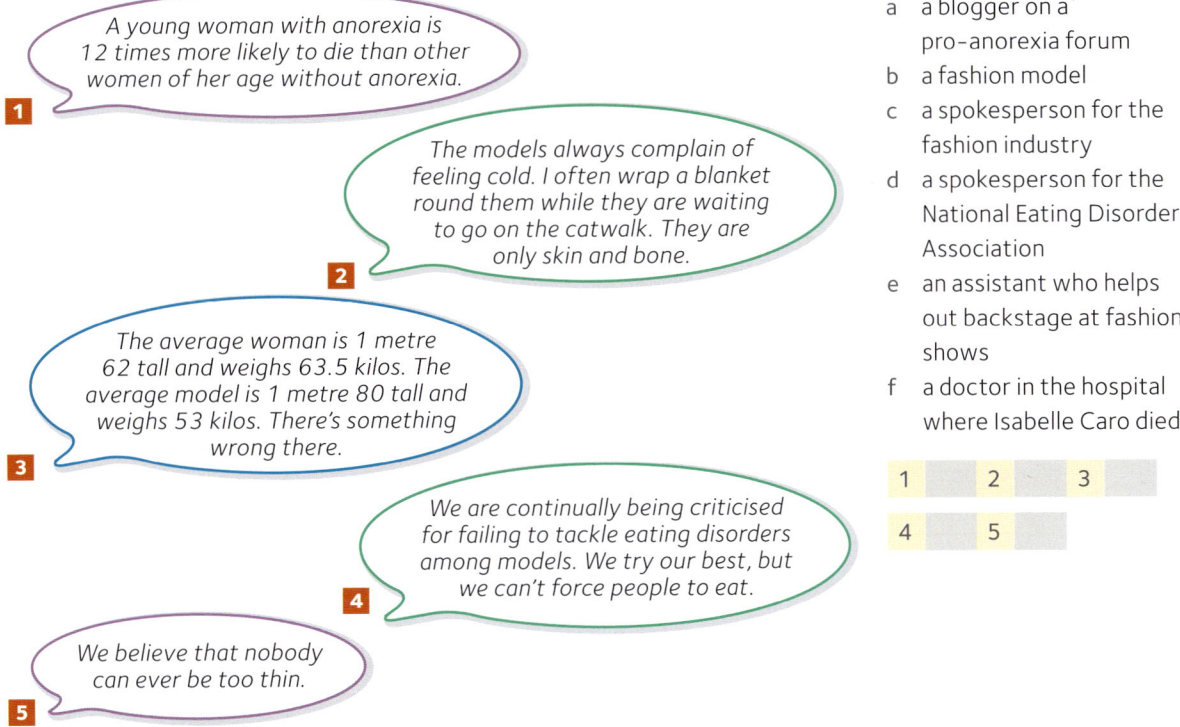

1 A young woman with anorexia is 12 times more likely to die than other women of her age without anorexia.

2 The models always complain of feeling cold. I often wrap a blanket round them while they are waiting to go on the catwalk. They are only skin and bone.

3 The average woman is 1 metre 62 tall and weighs 63.5 kilos. The average model is 1 metre 80 tall and weighs 53 kilos. There's something wrong there.

4 We are continually being criticised for failing to tackle eating disorders among models. We try our best, but we can't force people to eat.

5 We believe that nobody can ever be too thin.

a   a blogger on a pro-anorexia forum
b   a fashion model
c   a spokesperson for the fashion industry
d   a spokesperson for the National Eating Disorders Association
e   an assistant who helps out backstage at fashion shows
f   a doctor in the hospital where Isabelle Caro died

1		2		3	
4		5			

C Group the speakers above according to their position on extreme dieting. Say who is for and who is against very slim models.

for: _____   against: _____

3 **Reading: eating disorders among children and adolescents in Germany**

Read the text and decide if the statements that follow are true or false. Correct the false statements.

According to a recent study carried out in Germany, eating disorders are among the most common health problems among 11- to 17-year-olds. Almost 7,500 people in this age group completed a questionnaire which was designed to discover eating disorders. The questionnaire covered aspects such as Body Mass Index (BMI) and sexual and body self-image assessment. The study showed that girls are more frequently affected by eating disorders than boys. Another difference shown by the study was that, starting from age 11, more girls develop eating disorders as they age, while the number of boys who develop eating disorders drops from the age of 11. It seems that as girls grow older, they become more concerned with their body image, whereas boys become less interested.

		True	False
1	Over 7,500 children and adolescents in Germany have eating disorders.		
2	A questionnaire was specially developed in order to find out more about eating habits.		
3	The questionnaire contained questions about people's weight and how they feel about themselves.		
4	Both boys and girls are equally affected with eating disorders.		
5	Girls are more at risk of developing eating disorders as they become older.		
6	Boys become more interested in dieting as they get older.		

C The media – a blessing or a curse?

1 **Word power: dreams for sale**

A One word or phrase in each group *does not* make a strong collocation with the word in **bold**. Score out the word that does not fit.

1 **perfect** body • figure • health • participant • plan
2 **feeling** better • muscle • sexier • slow • sluggish
3 **healthy** calories • choice • exercise • meals • lifestyle
4 **fitness** choice • people • plan • programme • workout
5 **exercise** log • motivation • plan • programme • schedule
6 **daily** exercise • routine • schedule • strength • workout

B Rearrange the words below and add the correct form of *get* to make sentences you might read on health and fitness sites.

1 already / you / at home / some / vitamin supplements?

_____

2 did you feel / this morning / slow and sluggish / when you / up?

_____

3 as quickly / do you want to / as possible / the perfect body?

_____

4 celebrities do / in shape / just / like.

_____

5 and stay fit / in time for summer / our plan / will help you / fit.

_____

6 already / hope / on our 60-day plan / started / you / we.

_____

2 **Reading: messages in men's magazines**   > *Schwierige Texte lesen: SB p. 210*

A Read the article on the opposite page and select the correct summary of the text.

☐ 1 According to research, images in men's magazines are one of the main causes of eating disorders among young people.

☐ 2 Research among men aged between 18 and 36 indicates that they read men's magazines because they prefer the shapely figures of the women they see in them to the thin girls they see in everyday life.

☐ 3 Research suggests that younger men who read men's magazines could be psychologically harmed by the images of perfect male physiques they contain.

B Match the following German words and phrases to expressions in the text.

1 *es mit dem Training übertreiben* _____

2 *von Bildern beeinflusst werden* _____

3 *sich einen muskulären Körperbau erarbeiten* _____

4 *krankhafte Bessessenheit entwickeln* _____

5 *an einer Körperdysmorphen Störung (KDS) leiden* _____

6 *sich auf den eigenen Körperbau konzentrieren* _____

The influence of men's magazines

While magazines aimed at men often include pictures of sexy women, researcher Dr David Giles said images of male bodies shown in these magazines may be dangerous to men. His research indicated that regular readers of men's magazines were more likely to exercise to excess.

Giles surveyed 161 men aged between 18 and 36, and found that those who regularly read the magazines were more likely to be influenced by images of men shown on the pages. Apart from exercising, some of the readers said they were also more likely to consider using anabolic steroids to improve their appearance.

Dr Giles said: "The message in typical men's magazines is that you need to develop a muscular physique in order to attract good-looking women. Readers worry that their bodies are not good enough and this leads to desperate attempts to improve them. Both men and women get their ideas of what they should look like from the imagery they see in the media," he went on. "Young people in general are developing unhealthy obsessions about their own bodies."

The medical name for these unhealthy obsessions is body dysmorphic disorder, also called "athletica nervosa" by some specialists. Professor Naomi Fineberg, a consultant psychiatrist, said that men and women suffered equally from body dysmorphic disorder.

Professor Fineberg said: "Some men focus on their figures and do a lot of exercise in order to gain perfectly formed muscles. We can't say for sure whether these magazines are causing athletica nervosa," she said, "but these images may play a part in encouraging men to over-exercise."   (282 words)

abridged and adapted from news.bbc.co.uk

Too much exercise can be bad for you

C Write a German summary of the text in your notebook.

> Mediation: SB p. 219

3

Reading: a petition

Read Benjamin O'Keefe's online petition and match the two parts of the sentences.

1 Abercrombie & Fitch does not make clothes
2 Abercrombie & Fitch should make clothes
3 Abercrombie & Fitch is of the opinion that
4 Benjamin says that we should encourage
5 Benjamin thinks that young people already have enough problems
6 Benjamin wants Abercrombie & Fitch to treat young people

a with respect and produce suitable clothes for all.
b their clothes are not for everyone.
c for young people who are not attractive.
d young people to love the way they are.
e for all young people, whatever their shape and size.
f trying to meet society's idea of what is beautiful.

1		2		3		4		5		6	

To: Abercrombie and Fitch

Stop telling teens they aren't beautiful and start making clothes for young people of all shapes and sizes!

Mike Jeffries and Abercrombie & Fitch owe thousands of young people an apology! Mr. Jeffries has made his opinion very clear, if you don't fit his "cookie cutter" ideal image, he doesn't want you wearing his product.

"Candidly, we go after the cool kids. We go after the attractive all-American kid with a great attitude and a lot of friends. A lot of people don't belong [in our clothes], and they can't belong."

In a world where teens are constantly under pressure to fit the societal norms of beauty, we should be building them up and helping them love themselves who they are not blatantly telling them they don't belong.

It's time that Mike Jeffries issue a formal apology and Abercrombie starts to embrace and make products for all body types!

Yours sincerely,
[your name]

3 The perfect pitch

A A marketing meeting

1 **Describing charts** > *Schaubilder und Statistiken beschreiben und analysieren: SB p. 218*

Choose the best description for each of the charts 1–6. There is one description that you do not need.

a Sales rose steadily during the first half of the year.
b Sales fluctuated considerably during the year.
c Sales declined quickly but then surged at the end of the year.
d Sales declined slightly during the first half of the year, then increased rapidly.
e Sales dipped sharply in the middle of the year but then improved.
f Sales remained constant all year.
g Sales fluctuated considerably during the first half of the year then rose sharply.

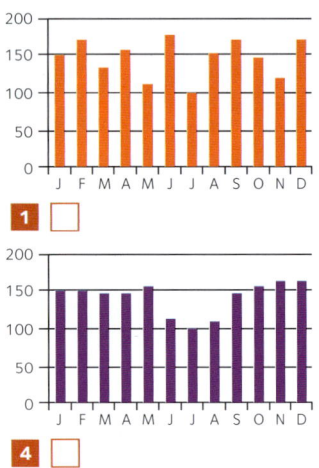

2 **Reported speech: talking about products** > *Reported speech: SB p. 227*

Rewrite the statements in reported speech.

1 Sally announced: "We're going to launch a new product." (Use *they*.)

_____

2 She said: "It's called the Zipper Neo."

_____

3 The engineering team said: "We have spent six months developing it."

_____

4 The press release stated: "Urban Wheels launched the Urban Zipper last year." (Use *the previous year*.)

_____

5 It claimed: "The Urban Zipper was the best scooter on the market at that time."

_____

6 The reviewer wrote: "The Zipper Neo has a longer range and more power."

_____

7 The advertisement claimed: "Teenagers will love it."

_____

8 Bob said: "Customers are already placing orders."

_____

3 **Listening: planning an agenda**

Sven and Sally are planning the agenda for the next marketing meeting. Listen to the conversation and complete the agenda.

URBAN
WHEELS

Marketing Meeting – Agenda

Date: _____

Time: _____

Chair: Sven Hoffmann

Invitees: Sales: Bob Carr (Director), Delphine Roussel (Regional Manager)

Marketing; Sally Truman (Director)

Product Development: Sven Hoffmann (Director), Felix Wagner (Urban Zipper Team Leader),

Heike König (Zipper Neo Team Leader), _____ (Junior Design Engineer)

Production: Aart Bakker (Manager)

	Topic	Leader		Topic	Leader
1	_____ _____	_____	**2**	_____ _____	_____
1.1	_____ _____	_____	2.1	_____ _____	_____
1.2	_____ _____	_____	2.2	_____ _____	_____
1.3	_____ _____	_____	2.3	_____ _____	_____
1.4	_____ _____	_____	2.4	_____ _____	
3	_____ _____	_____			
4	_____ _____				

> *Mit Hör- / Sehverstehensaufgaben umgehen: SB p. 215*

1   **Mediation: YouTube marketing**

Sie finden diesen Artikel im Internet und möchten den Inhalt Ihren deutschsprachigen Kolleginnen und Kollegen vermitteln. Fassen Sie folgende Aspekte auf Deutsch in einer E-Mail zusammen. Übersetzen Sie dabei nicht Wort für Wort.

- Das Potential von YouTube als Marketingwerkzeug
- Warum manche Firmen bei YouTube keinen Erfolg haben
- Warum "Channels" (Kanäle) wichtig sind und wie man sie verwenden sollte

Using YouTube to market your business

1 YouTube is the world's most used online video hosting service. Did you know that people upload around 100 hours of video to YouTube every minute? If you want a video on any subject, from cute cats and clever dogs to how to ride a motorcycle or build a rocket motor, YouTube is the place to look for it.

2 Beside every video on YouTube is a list of "suggested videos" – other videos on related subjects. Just like other forms of social media, YouTube encourages users to be interactive: they can express their opinions about videos, store videos to watch later, embed them in their own websites and blogs and share them with friends. As a result of all these communication tools, videos can become popular in hours, and previously unknown people can become celebrities overnight thanks to the "viral effect".

3 All of this means that YouTube has great potential as a marketing tool for businesses. You could use YouTube to launch or promote products, get feedback from potential customers, provide customer service and encourage your customers to share their good opinion of your business.

4 However, the sheer size of YouTube makes it confusing to many businesses. How can your company organize its video content so that it does not get lost among the millions of other videos? For every video that "goes viral", there are thousands which get few views, no "likes" and no "shares".

5 The best way to make sure that your videos are easy to find is to set up a YouTube "channel". This is a place to bring all of your videos together and organize them. You can also customize your channel with your company logo to give it a brand personality. Even better: you can provide company information and a link to your website in the "About" section of your channel.

6 Best of all, YouTube viewers can subscribe to your channel, so that they are informed when you upload new content to it. Subscribing to a channel is similar to "liking" and "following" a company on Facebook – it creates a dialogue between the company and the potential customer.

❯ *Mediation: SB p. 219*

2 **Word power: online merketing**

Match the following German words and phrases to expressions in the text on page 18.

1 soziale Medien ___Sogiar media___

2 seine Meinung ausdrücken ___express their opinion___

3 einbinden ___embed___

4 Kommunikationsmittel ___communication tools___

5 auf den Markt bringen ___launch products___

6 Kundendienst ___customer service___

7 individuell aufmachen ___customize___

8 abonnieren ___subscribe___

3 **Watching a video: Scrooser**

2

Watch the video and decide if the following statements are true or false. Use information from the video to correct the false statements.

		True	False
1	Scrooser's marketing department invented the phrase "Harley Davidson for the sidewalk".		
2	The Scrooser is light enough to carry.		
3	Style isn't very important to the Scrooser team.		
4	Even the designers are surprised by how smoothly the Scrooser moves.		
5	The Scrooser adapts to the rider's riding style.		
6	Scrooser is looking for business partners to help finance the project.		

4 **Word power: describing a product**

Your company has decided to promote the Urban Zipper by making a YouTube video. Complete the video narrator's script with the expressions from the box.

> energy-efficient electric motor • exciting innovation • intelligent solution • lightweight frame •
> precision engineering • rigorous testing • silent electric motor • standards of excellence •
> urban mobility • urban environment

The Urban Zipper is an _____[1] in modern city transport. For true

_____[2] in our busy cities, you need to use a combination of public transport

and personal transport. The Urban Zipper was built for the _____[3].

Its _____[4] means that you can easily carry it on buses, trams and trains.

Its _____[5] means that it will run and run for kilometre after kilometre.

But the Urban Zipper was built for fun and relaxation, too. Just imagine cruising through a city park – the

Zipper's _____[6] will allow you to enjoy the wind in your hair and the birds

singing in the trees. Its high quality German _____[7] is completely reliable,

completely safe. The Zipper is built to the highest _____[8]. After months of

_____[9], we're confident that the Neo is almost unbreakable under normal street

conditions. The Urban Zipper – it's the _____[10] to getting around the city!

1 **Mediation: product review**

You find this product review of the Urban Zipper in a German magazine. Summarize the main points in English for your non-German colleagues:

- things that the reviewer likes
- things that the reviewer dislikes or sees as faults
- the reviewer's general impression
- other Urban Wheels products mentioned

In the box are some words that you can use.

chassis	*Fahrgestell*
fold up	*zusammenklappen*
compact	*kompakt*
manoeuvrability	*Wendigkeit*
sporty	*sportlich*
seat	*Sitz*
highly priced	*in gehobener Preislage*
luxury	*Luxus*
press release	*Pressemitteilung*

ROAD TEST

> **Urban Zipper**
> von Urban Wheels GmbH
> 1.190 € (unverbindliche Preisempfehlung)

Keine Frage: Der Urban Zipper von Urban Wheels GmbH ist eine ausgezeichnete Maschine. Der effiziente 1kW-Motor treibt diesen Elektrotretroller mit 25 Stundenkilometern voran, auch wenn der Rollerfahrer wie ich 90 Kilo leicht und 35 Jahre jung ist.

Das Fahrgestell ist robust und dabei erstaunlich leicht, weil aus Titan: Der Roller hat ein Gesamtgewicht von 18 Kilo einschließlich der Lithium-Batterie. Er lässt sich blitzschnell zusammenklappen und (bei einiger Muskelkraft) problemlos mittragen, wenn man den Bus oder die Bahn nehmen will. Auch beim täglichen Gequetsche in der U-Bahn ist der kompakte, zusammengeklappte Roller kein großes Hindernis.

Trotzdem gibt es am Konzept einiges auszusetzen. Jüngere Fahrerinnen und Fahrer werden mehr Power und mehr Wendigkeit verlangen: Sportlich ist dieser Roller nicht gerade, also doch schon eher was für *Commuters* (Pendlerinnen und Pendler). Die Firma nennt den Urban Zipper also zu Recht einen *Commuter Scooter*.

Allerdings: Wenn der Urban Zipper ein Pendlerroller sein soll, dann ist ein bequemer Sitz vonnöten – der Zipper hat gar keinen. Zu wenig Komfort für Pendler und zu wenig Sportlichkeit für Teenager? Außerdem ist dieser Elektroroller bei fast 1.200 Euro in gehobener Preislage, da erwartet man schon mehr Luxus.

Die Kids (ja, wir alten „Kids" auch) bekommen aber bald ihren eigenen, sportlicheren Zipper, denn einer Pressemitteilung zufolge bringt Urban Wheels bald einen neuen Elektroroller auf den Markt: Leistungsstärker, leichter und wendiger als der Urban Zipper soll der neue Zipper Neo sein. Ich freue mich schon auf eine Probefahrt.

Gesamtbewertung: gut

2   **FAB analysis**

Urban Wheels decides to offer the following accessories with the Zipper range of electric scooters. Match the features, advantages and benefits to the products 1–5.

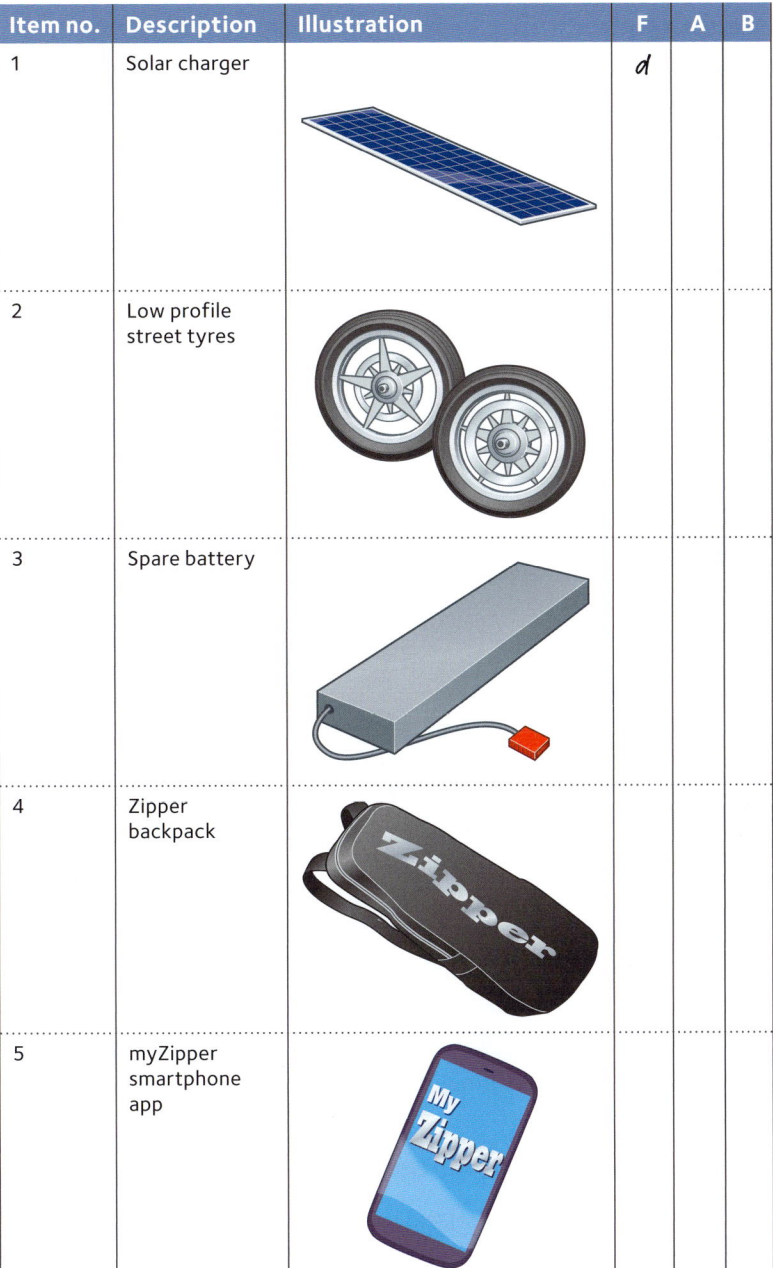

Item no.	Description	Illustration	F	A	B
1	Solar charger		d		
2	Low profile street tyres				
3	Spare battery				
4	Zipper backpack				
5	myZipper smartphone app				

Features

a   It allows you to lock and unlock your Zipper remotely and track your Zipper on Google Maps if someone steals it.

b   It delivers an extra 2,000 Watts of power

c   It has been specially designed to carry your folded Zipper scooter.

d   It converts sunlight to electricity.

e   They are suitable for use on roads or footpaths.

Advantages

f   Carry your Zipper easily on public transport

g   It gives you 45 km more range.

h   They are more energy efficient than our standard tyres on city streets.

i   You can charge your Zipper anywhere when the sun is shining.

j   You don't need a key or a bike lock.

Benefits

k   Don't worry about running out of power.

l   Go further and faster on the road.

m   Go further and help the environment.

n   Know that your Zipper will always be there.

o   Use buses and trains without stress.

3   **Writing: a press release**

Write a press release for the Zipper Facebook page using your answers to exercise 2. Start like this:

> Breaking news: Urban Wheels is excited to announce a new range of accessories to make your ZIPPER experience even more special. So – ZIP to our online store now and place your order!
>
> Do you want to go further and help the environment? Well now you can: the specially designed Zipper solar charger …

A Meet the family

 1

Word power: family members

A Sort the words from the box into the family tree.

> aunt • brother • cousins • daughter • father • grandfather • grandmother • grandson • half-sister • mother • nephew • sister • sister-in-law • son • son-in-law • stepbrother • stepfather • wife

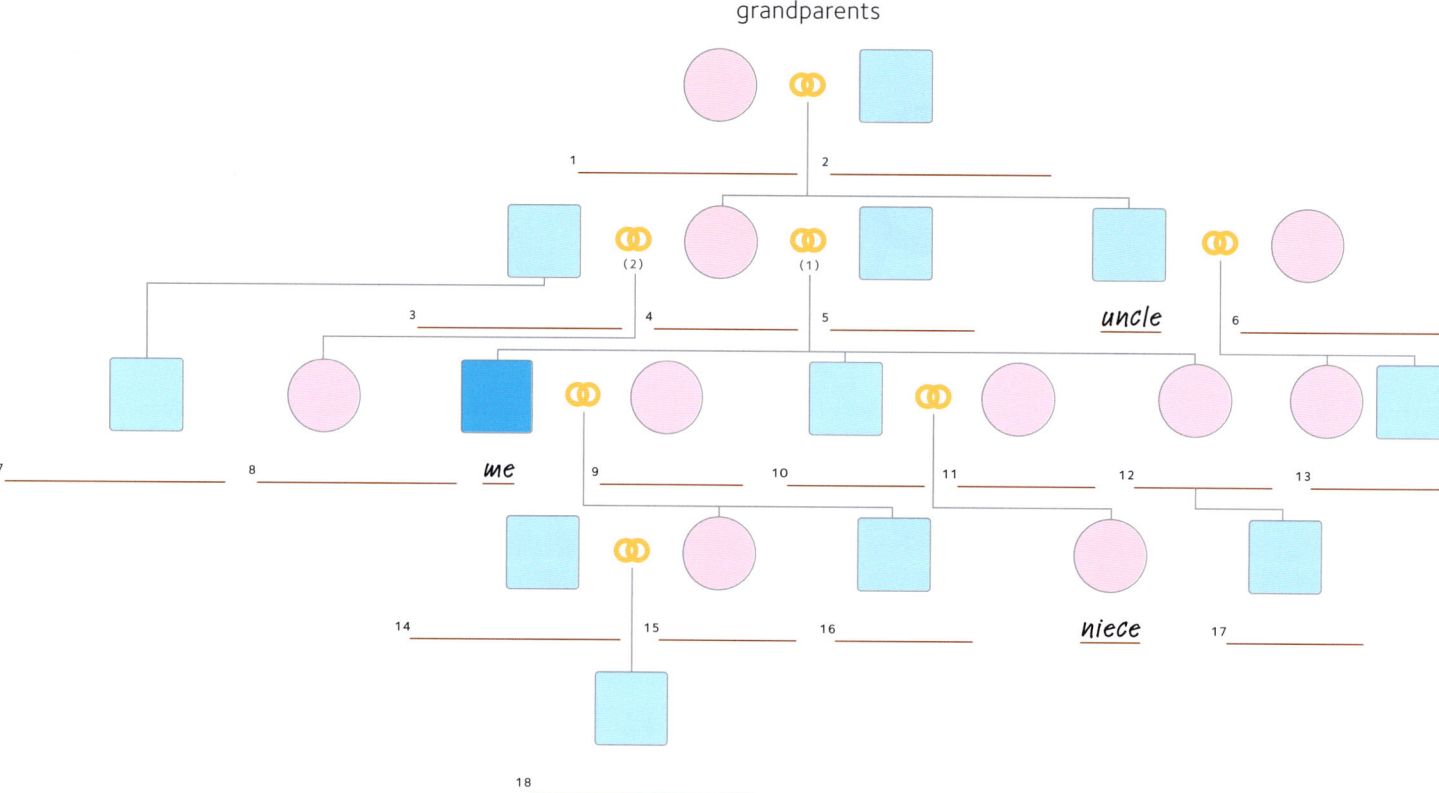

B Use the English equivalents of the phrases in brackets to complete the descriptions of the family set-ups below.

1 A _____ (*Familie mit (nur) einem Elternteil*) is a family in which a person takes care of their child or children without a husband, wife or partner.

2 A _____ (*Kernfamilie*) is one that consists of father, mother and children.

3 A _____ (*Stieffamilie*) is a family that is formed when somebody marries or moves in with a person who already has children.

4 An _____ (*interkulturelle Familie*) is a family in which the parents are from different cultures.

5 A _____ (*Einwandererfamilie*) is a family in which the parents or grandparents originally came from another country.

6 An _____ (*erweiterte Familie*) is a family group with a close relationship among the members that include not only parents and children but also uncles, aunts, grandparents, etc.

2

Describing change: the British Royal Family

> *Simple past: SB p. 223; Present perfect: SB p. 224*

Complete the extract from a magazine with the simple past or present perfect form of the verbs in brackets.

Like many families in Britain, the British Royal Family _____ (change)[1] with the times. As well as births and marriages, the family _____ (have)[2] quite a few divorces. 1992 _____ (be)[3] a horrible year for Queen Elizabeth. In March, her second son Andrew and his wife Sarah _____ (split up)[4] ; in April of the same year, her daughter Anne, _____ (leave)[5] her husband and in December, the British government _____ (announce)[6] the separation of Elizabeth's oldest son Charles and his wife Diana.

The British people _____ (become)[7] angry when they _____ (learn)[8] about Charles's affair with his childhood sweetheart, Camilla. Things _____ (get worse)[9] in 1997, when Diana _____ (die)[10] in a car crash in Paris. Immediately after the accident,

when the Royal Family _____ (remain)[11] in their holiday castle in Scotland, many people _____ (think)[12] the Queen was a cold-hearted mother-in-law. Later, she _____ (appear)[13] on British TV and _____ (say)[14] some kind words about her dead daughter-in-law and _____ (speak)[15] "as a grandmother" about her concern for her grandsons, William and Harry.

And how do things look now? Since 2000, there _____ (be)[16] more marriages than divorces, starting with Charles and Camilla's in 2005. More recently, William _____ (marry)[17] his college sweetheart Kate. The young couple _____ (give)[18] Queen Elizabeth her first great grandson, a boy who might one day be king. We wonder what the Royal Family will look like then.

3

Watching a video: "Just a family"

> *Mit Hör- und Sehverstehensaufgaben umgehen: SB p. 215*

3

What do you remember about Heather Greenwood and her family? Decide if the following statements are true or false, and correct the false statements. Then watch and check.

		True	False
1	Heather was adopted by a mixed-race couple.		
2	Her family has become racially diverse through adoption, marriage and birth.		
3	Heather and Dolores had no difficulties as young mothers of mixed-race children.		
4	Heather's father, Ed, felt sad when his children experienced racism.		
5	When Heather is out with her family, no one notices that her children are biracial.		
6	Heather would be unhappy if one of her children fell in love with someone of a different race.		
7	Heather's husband is proud of his family.		

1 Word power: talking about dysfunctional families

A Use a dictionary to complete the word families table. Nine of the words that already appear in the table can be found on page 48 of the Student's Book.

noun	verb	adjective
abuse	_____ 1	_____ 2
adultery	…	_____ 3
alcoholism	…	_____ 4
battering	_____ 5	_____ 6
_____ 7 _____ 8	to lie	…
manipulation _____ 9	_____ 10	manipulative
_____ 11	to neglect	neglectful _____ 12
promiscuity	…	_____ 13
victim	_____ 14	_____ 15

B Complete the sentences using the correct form of the words above.

1 She always manages to get me to do things I don't want to do. It is very sad that she has grown up to be so

_____ .

2 When I asked her where she was going, she told me a _____ . She said she was going

out with her sister but I knew she was meeting another man.

3 Mary seems to go from one _____ relationship into another. Her new boyfriend is

even more violent than the last one.

4 As a child, she was always covered in bruises. Her father used to _____ her regularly.

She was _____ at school because of her family background.

5 Jo was having sex with his secretary, so his wife divorced him for

_____ . He has always been very

_____ .

6 The parents are both suffering from _____ and

often forget about their children. Their drinking has become so bad that

the social services have removed the _____

children from the family home.

2   **Adverbs of frequency: How often …?**

> Adverbs of frequency: SB p. 233

A   Place the adverbs from the box on the scale below.

> *always • frequently • never • often • sometimes • usually*

0%	40%	60%	80%	90%	100%

B   Complete the sentences by ticking (✓) the correct position for the adverb in brackets.

1   The parents ☐ leave the children at home alone ☐ when they go to the pub. (sometimes)

2   They ☐ are ☐ away for hours. (often)

3   Does she ☐ look after the younger children ☐ when her mother is drunk? (always)

4   What does the family ☐ do ☐ when the police come around? (usually)

5   The father ☐ is ☐ aggressive. (frequently)

6   The baby is ☐ covered ☐ in bruises. (sometimes)

7   The girl ☐ has ☐ any breakfast before she goes to school. (never)

---

3   **Describing a case**

> Simple present: SB p. 222; Simple past: SB p. 223; Present perfect: SB p. 224

Choose the correct form of the verbs to complete the case notes.

Cathy P., who (is / was / has been)[1] born on 29 April, 20..,

(comes / came / has come)[2] to our women's refuge at 4.30 p.m.

Ms P. (bring / brought / has brought)[3] her six-year-old twin

daughters with her. Ms P. (describes / described / has described)[4]

how her husband (beats / beat / has beaten)[5] her earlier in the

afternoon. Ms P. (has / had / has had)[6] a black eye and she

(shows / showed / has shown)[7] me a number of old bruises on her

back and arms. According to Ms P., her husband (never beats /

never beat / has never beaten)[8] the twins. There (is / was /

has been)[9] no sign that the twins (are / were / have been)[10] physically abused. In our

conversation this evening, Ms P. (tells / told / has told)[11] me that the beatings (start / started /

have started)[12] just after the twins (are / were / have been)[13] born. When I (ask / asked / have asked)[14]

her why she (never looks for / never looked for / has never looked for)[15] assistance until now, she (says /

said / has said)[16] that she (is / was / has been)[17] too frightened. Ms P. and the twins (are / were /

have been)[18] asleep in room 22 now.

C Making decisions

1 **Word power: describing the case of a pregnant teenager**

Read the words and phrases in the box and sort them under the headings below.

> abortion • adoption agency • antenatal clinic • counsellor • family support team • keep the baby •
> the father of the baby • give up the baby for adoption • the mother's family • potential adoptive couples •
> social worker • teenage mother • termination

Professionals involved in the case	Other people involved in the case	Options
_____	_____	_____
_____	_____	_____
_____	_____	_____
_____	_____	_____
_____	_____	_____

2 **Describing a case**

A Match the sentence halves to make complete sentences about a case.

1 ☐ Linda M., who is 18 years old,
2 ☐ Linda's family doctor referred her to us and has supplied
3 ☐ Linda lives in an extended family
4 ☐ She says that her family is very close
5 ☐ She has not told the father of her baby
6 ☐ Linda is realistic about her situation
7 ☐ We have referred Linda to the hospital
8 ☐ Linda understands that she must wait for three days
9 ☐ The client knows that

a   a pregnancy certificate.
b   and given her a certificate of counselling.
c   and also very religious.
d   and says that at the moment she is not ready to have a baby.
e   between counselling and the operation.
f   with her parents, two sisters and one grandparent.
g   is in the 10th week of a pregnancy.
h   that she is pregnant.
i   she can come back to us at any time if she needs further counselling.

B Adapt the information from exercise 2A to complete the case notes using the headings below. Write full sentences in your notebook and use your own words as often as possible.

Case # 37622

The client
Linda M. is 18 years old. She is 10 weeks pregnant. She was referred to us by ...

The family background

Client's assessment of the situation

The current situation

3 Reading: three assessments of potential adopters

Complete the case notes with words and phrases from the boxes. In each box, there is one more phrase than you need.

birth certificates • considering adoption •
fertility treatment • infertile • older mothers •
recommend • suitable adoptive parents •
the social services

adopted • candidates for adoption •
keen to adopt • passive smoking • referred •
selection process • well looked after •
wife and mother

Case 1

Lisa and Jim C. are a healthy couple in their early 40s. They have secure jobs; both work in _____ [1]. They have been trying for many years to have a child. Both partners have had tests which show that they are not _____ [2] but they have given up the idea of ever having children of their own. The couple was offered _____ [3] recently but they say they are not keen on the idea. Ms C. has read about risks for _____ [4]. The couple is now _____ [5]. After assessment, we feel we can _____ [6] them as _____ [7].

Case 2

Mary and John M. are both in their late 30s. Mr M. is a policeman, Mrs M. is a full-time _____ [1]. The couple have five children, three of their own and two who are _____ [2]. All of the children are healthy and _____ [3]. Mr and Mrs M. are _____ [4] another child. The couple explained that their oldest child (aged 17) is a smoker. The couple and their son understand the risks of _____ [5] to babies and young children. We have _____ [6] them to a programme which helps teenagers stop smoking and asked them to get in touch when their son has completed the programme. Mr and Mrs M understand that they have to go through the _____ [7] again.

agency recommendations • application to adopt • autoimmune disease • community service •
convicted • criminal record • social worker

Case 3

Jane L. and Mike K. are in their mid-twenties. Mr K. has an _____ [1] which may be passed on to any children he may have. Ms L. was _____ [2] for stealing a packet of spaghetti from a supermarket one year ago. She successfully completed six months of _____ [3]. We have explained that Ms L.'s _____ [4] should not make a difference to the couple's _____ [5]. However, we have asked Ms L. to submit a report from the _____ [6] who dealt with her case last year.

A Teams for teens

1 **Word power: the Outreach website**

Complete the crossword puzzle with one-word answers. You will find the words in the text on page 195 of the Student's Book.

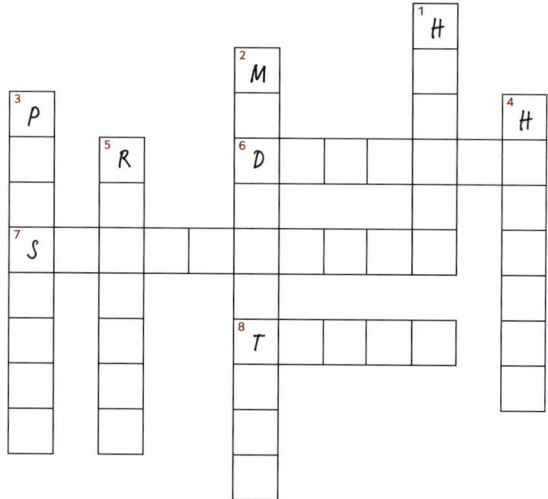

ACROSS:
6 A sense of your own importance and value
7 When you think that sb has done sth wrong, but you have no proof, you are …
8 Belief that sb is reliable and honest

DOWN:
1 Things people do often, without thinking, especially things that are hard to stop doing
2 A drug or drugs you take to deal with an illness
3 To make sb agree to do sth by giving them good reasons for doing it: to…
4 The practice of keeping yourself clean
5 A feeling of admiration for sb because of their good qualities or achievements

2 **Talking about regular activities, current activities and plans**

Complete the dialogues with the simple present or present progressive form of the verb in brackets.

1

(A) What _____ (you do)¹ at Outreach, Mary?

(B) I _____ (look after)² teenagers who _____ (have)³ problems with substance abuse. At the moment, I _____ (write)⁴ some notes for the presentation I _____ (give)⁵ next week.

2

(A) _____ (Ian and Patsy be)¹ in the Outreach bus every day?

(B) Well, Ian _____ (be)², but Patsy only _____ (work)³ in the bus twice a week. This week, she _____ (go out)⁴ with the bus tomorrow and the day after.

3

(A) The trainees _____ (hold)¹ a workshop on Tuesday afternoon and they _____ (need)² a big room. _____ (you use)³ the group therapy room on Tuesday, Ahmed?

(B) You're in luck. I _____ (take)⁴ the group to the cinema then so I won't need the room.

4

(A) Who _____ (work)¹ in the media centre? The video _____ (run)² but nobody _____ (watch)³ it.

(B) Fiona _____ (not be)⁴ in there? She _____ (always help out)⁵ on Friday mornings.

> Simple present: SB p. 222; Present progressive: SB p. 222; The future: SB p. 225

3

Word power: at an Outreach centre

Sort the words and phrases below under the headings to make two lists.

advice • alcohol dependant • an anger management programme • at risk • education programmes •
from dysfunctional families • "get clean" programmes • homeless • shelters • somewhere they can go •
suffering from mental health problems • support • troubled • using drugs

Outreach looks after teenagers who are …   Outreach offers …

_____   _____

_____   _____

_____   _____

_____   _____

_____   _____

_____   _____

4

Mediation: the difficulties of living on the streets

› Mediation: SB p. 219

A Match the German words to the English translations.

1	*Obdachlosigkeit*	a	being moved on
2	*Vorräte*	b	homelessness
3	*Privatsphäre*	c	public places
4	*Habseligkeiten*	d	restrictions
5	*Einschränkungen*	e	supplies
6	*geklaut*	f	stolen
7	*Vertreibung*	g	privacy
8	*öffentliche Plätze*	h	possessions

1		2		3		4		5		6		7		8	

B A social worker from Outreach Cardiff is interested in what homeless teenagers say about living on the streets in Germany. Tell her what these teens say about their life. You can use some of the words from exercise 4A if you want.

„Das Leben auf der Straße ist sehr teuer. Es gibt keine Möglichkeit, zu kochen oder Vorräte zu lagern. Auf der Straße zu leben heißt auch, keine Privatsphäre und ganz wenig Eigentum zu haben. Manchmal werden unsere Habseligkeiten von anderen Wohnungslosen geklaut. Wer im Winter draußen schläft, kann leicht krank werden. Es gibt Übernachtungseinrichtungen, aber unsere Hunde sind dort nicht will-kommen. Es gibt überall Einschränkungen. Vertreibung gehört zum Alltag. Wir werden ständig von öffentlichen Plätzen weggeschickt. Jugendliche, die sich in Gruppen treffen, sind nicht gerne gesehen."

B Drug facts and figures

1

> Words for describing graphs: SB p. 139

Word power: describing graphs

Match the words and phrases (1–8) to the graphs (a–h). Use each expression only once. You can use a dictionary if you want.

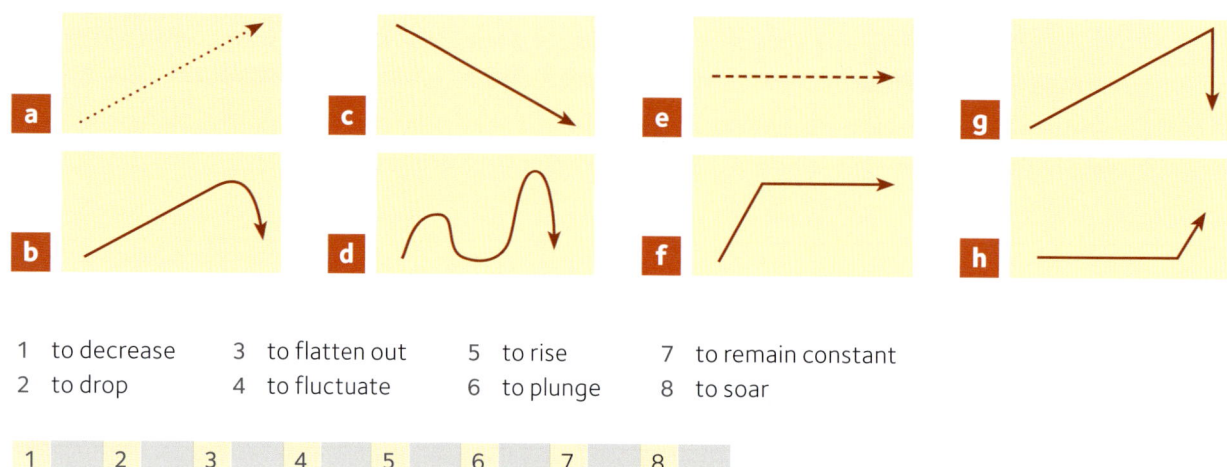

| a | c | e | g |

| b | d | f | h |

| 1 | to decrease | 3 | to flatten out | 5 | to rise | 7 | to remain constant |
| 2 | to drop | 4 | to fluctuate | 6 | to plunge | 8 | to soar |

| 1 | | 2 | | 3 | | 4 | | 5 | | 6 | | 7 | | 8 | |

2

> Schaubilder und Statistiken beschreiben und analysieren: SB p. 218

Describing a graph

Read the information, then complete the description of the graph with words from the box.

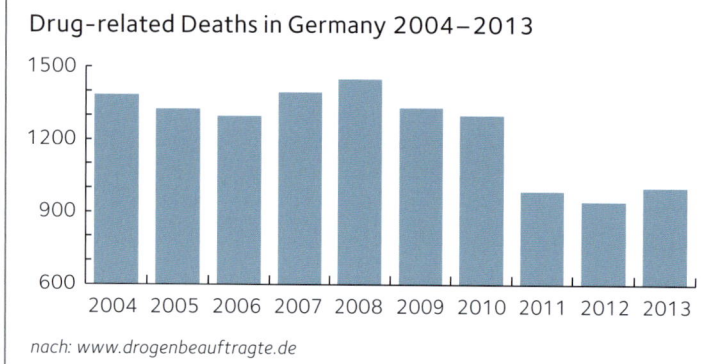

Drug-related Deaths in Germany 2004–2013

y-axis values: 1500, 1200, 900, 600

x-axis values: 2004 2005 2006 2007 2008 2009 2010 2011 2012 2013

nach: www.drogenbeauftragte.de

According to the latest statistics of the German Federal Criminal Police Office (*Bundeskriminalamt*) and the Federal Government's commissioner for drug-related issues (*Drogenbeauftragte der Bundesregierung*), the number of drug-related deaths in Germany rose again for the first time since 2008. As before, one of the main causes of death was the use of heroin.

---

from 2004 to 2013 • decreased slightly • higher level • increased • just under • plunged • remained constant • the number of deaths • the years

---

The graph shows the number of drug-related deaths in Germany _____¹.

The x-axis shows _____² and the y-axis gives _____³.

In 2004, there was a total of 1385 drug-related deaths in Germany. The number of deaths dropped to around 1300 in 2005 and to _____⁴ 1300 in 2006. In 2007, the number of deaths began to increase and reached a slightly _____⁵ than that reached in 2004. The number of drug-related deaths _____⁶ again in 2008 to a total of 1449.

In 2009, the number of deaths dropped to around 1300, and these figures _____⁷ in 2010. In 2011, numbers _____⁸ to an all-time low of 940. In 2012, numbers once again _____⁹. In 2013, the total rose for the first time since 2008, to 1000.

3

Reading: substance abuse and teenage homelessness

› Schwierige Texte lesen: SB p. 210

A Complete the text with words and phrases from the box. There are five words more than you need.

abuse • abusing • addiction • addictive • conflicts • dependency • dependent • peer pressure •
regular • regularity • substance • substantial • users

As several studies have shown, there is a relationship between substance abuse and homelessness among

teenagers. Substance _____¹ may start off as a result of _____² amongst

children as young as eight who encourage each other to try a cigarette. At an older age, alcohol comes into the

picture, and the cigarette may become a joint.

For many teenagers, the danger of slipping into _____³ is relatively slight. For those of them who

do become addicted, however, substance abuse may lead to a period of homelessness.

In a study carried out among homeless teenagers in England and Wales, 73% were found to be

_____⁴ drug users, using every day or week. A majority of them had left home, or had been thrown

out of the family home, because of family _____⁵ resulting from the teenagers' substance abuse.

Among the heroin and/or cocaine _____⁶, more than half only started to use these drugs after

becoming homeless. Many said that peer pressure had got them started.

In London, 83% of homeless teenagers were found to be _____⁷ abusers, whether of alcohol or

drugs, or both. Their levels of _____⁸ and the likelihood of them using "hard"

drugs increased the longer the teenagers remained homeless. (203 words)

B Read the text again and answer the following questions. Use your own words as often as possible.

1 Who might be the first person who suggests that a child or a teenager should try out a drug?
2 How might drug use develop after someone has tried their first drug?
3 What is the percentage of regular drug users among homeless teenagers in England and Wales?
4 What had led to most of them losing their home?
5 What can be the next step in drug use after a young person has become homeless?
6 How are things likely to continue with long-term homeless teenagers who are using drugs?

4

Word power: forming nouns

Sort the noun form of the verbs in the box into the
right category. Use a dictionary if you want.

believe • continue • ~~decrease~~ • develop • drop •
encourage • lose • relate •
result • start • suggest

same form as verb	with -ion ending	with -ment ending	irregular
decrease			

C Internet addiction

1 **Word power: internet addiction**

A Write the correct preposition in the gaps.

1 Mary was nearly knocked _____ when she crossed the road while playing Bubble Island on her phone.

2 Because he had spent so much time surfing the internet, John's phone bill was €600. He was left

_____ no money at then end of the month.

3 Every day Frank tried to sneak _____ from school a few times to go to an internet café to check his Facebook status.

4 The only thing Mike is frightened _____ is his computer crashing. He says his world would be in ruins if that happened.

5 A real internet addict does not even break _____ meals: he just eats snacks in front of the computer.

6 I am not addicted _____ computer gaming. I can stop when I want to, I just don't want to!

7 Since he started playing computer games, Mark shows no interest _____ anything but his computer.

8 My brother spends too much time _____ home playing computer games.

B Match the words with their definitions. All of them can be found in the text on page 62 of the Student's Book.

1	virtual	a	the legal ending of a marriage
2	obsession	b	leave a place secretly and without permission
3	issue	c	to do with to electro communications
4	divorce	d	interrupt what you are doing
5	sneak away	e	subject for discussion or argument
6	break	f	a thought, feeling or habit that a person cannot let go of

1		4	
2		5	
3		6	

2 **A cry for help and an answer**

Joseph believes he has a problem and has decided to find help online. Put his request and the answer he received in the right order.

Internet Addiction Support Group   [HOME]   [FORUM]   [CONTACT US]

Question

a At first I only played once or twice a day for about 2–3 hours.

b I am 17 and a STAR DOME addict. My parents worry about my obsession, but never try to stop me from playing.

c But now I play about 8–10 hours a day, both before school and well into the night. I feel this game is controlling me, but I can't stop. I need help.

d Sometimes they suggest I go outside, but I can't. I have no life. I can't even imagine what I would do if I deleted my games account. I really want to quit but I don't know how.

Response

e But don't worry, video game addiction can be treated. Identifying the problem is part of the solution.

f This is why it will take it will take a lot of effort to find interests and activities to replace video games. You may also require outside help, such as a therapist or treatment program, if there are underlying problems that led to the game obsession in the first place.

g Tell them that, as with any other addictions, you may resist change and have withdrawal symptoms.

h I am happy that you have approached me with this problem. I suggest you tell your parents directly that they need to help you.

Question: ☐ ☐ ☐ ☐   Response: ☐ ☐ ☐ ☐

3

Listening: the dangers of internet addiction

5

A Before you listen to Maggie Wang, find the collocations she uses to talk about the dangers of internet addiction. Then listen and check.

1	breathing	a	air
2	coping	b	exercise
3	everyday	c	interaction
4	let off	d	life
5	social	e	network
6	support	f	problem
7	thin	g	skills
8	underlying	h	steam

1	____	5	____
2	____	6	____
3	____	7	____
4	____	8	____

B Use the collocations you found in 3A to complete the following sentences.

1   When things escalated, Bob showed his _____ and managed to deal with the situation.

2   My mother only knows one way to _____ when life gets too much for her: she shouts at everybody!

3   The _____ of Colin's internet addiction was his poor self-esteem.

4   If you are feeling stressed, _____ can help to calm you down and let you deal with matters more easily.

5   In a good family _____ , the family members help and support one another.

6   An addiction will not suddenly vanish into _____ . The addict has to be pro-active.

7   People sometimes become addicted to the internet when they feel that their _____ is not exciting enough.

8   Spending hours on the internet means a person is missing real face-to-face _____ .

4

Describing a cartoon

Study the cartoon, then choose the best sentence endings to complete the interpretation.

1   The man pictured in the cartoon

a   works in the Internet Addiction Therapy Clinic. ☐

b   is probably an internet addict. ☐

c   only uses his email address when absolutely necessary. ☐

2   The impression is created by the

a   woman who is looking for new friends. ☐

b   sad look on his face and signboard on the wall. ☐

c   colour of the man's shirt. ☐

3   The message of the cartoon seems to be that

a   it is impossible to escape the internet. ☐

b   not everyone has an email address. ☐

c   addicts can be very forgetful. ☐

33

6 A problem shared

A Listening between the lines

1 **Word power: talking about abuse**

A Complete the text with words and phrases from the box.

> isolation • victim • afraid • signs and symptoms • cuts and bruises • abuser •
> suicidal • physical violence • self-esteem • accident

As caring professionals, we have to be aware that anyone, whoever they are, can be a _____¹ of

abuse. It is important that we recognize the _____². In general, if someone seems

_____³ or anxious to please their partner, then their partner could be an _____⁴ of

some kind. If your client continually has _____⁵, and says every time that these

injuries are the result of an _____⁶, that client may be a victim of _____⁷.

A victim of emotional abuse is likely to have very low _____⁸ and he/she could also depressed or

_____⁹. Keeping a victim away from friends and family is also a type of abuse. One of the warning

signs of _____¹⁰ is missing social occasions without an excuse.

B Describe the cycle of violence in domestic abuse. Draw a line between the six steps in the cycle. The first line has been drawn for you.

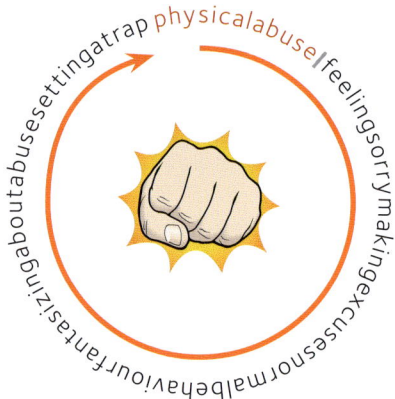

physicalabuse|feelingsorrymakingexcusesnormalbehaviourfantasizingaboutabusesettingatrap

C Complete the grid with phrases from exercise 1B. Add other words and phrases to expand the descriptions. Try to do this without looking at the slides on page 71 of the Student's Book.

1	The cycle of abuse starts with	*physical abuse such as hitting, punching and/or kicking.*
2	When the abuser has had enough, he/she starts	
3	The next step in the cycle is	
4	After that, there is a period of	
5	Next, the abuser starts	
6	The final step is	

2   **Describing behaviour: five scenes from an abusive relationship**   > *Adjectives and adverbs: SB p. 232*

A   Complete these conversations with adjectives or adverbs. Strike through the words that don't fit.

Scene 1: At work

Boss: Why do you have a scarf tied so (tight / tightly)[1] round your neck again, Mandy?

Mandy: I have a cold and I don't feel very (good / well)[2].

Boss: Last week, you were wearing (dark / darkly)[3] glasses and I heard you crying (quiet / quietly)[4] in the ladies' room. Would you like to tell me anything?

Mandy: I was just a bit (unhappy / unhappily)[5] that day, that's all.

Scene 2: In the street

Mrs A: The Millers were arguing (loud / loudly)[1] again yesterday.

Mrs B: Did Mandy leave the house (quick / quickly)[2] after the argument as usual?

Mrs A: Yes, she did. She looked (bad / badly)[3] .

Mrs B: That poor girl. Bill Miller is a very (aggressive / aggressively)[4] man.

Scene 3: At the marriage guidance counsellor

Mandy: I'm sorry that Bill is (late / lately)[1] for our appointment. He's been busy (late / lately)[2].

Counsellor: You said that he has a very (stressful / stressfully)[3] job.

Mandy: That's right. He really would like to come (regular / regularly)[4] to our meetings but, as I said before, it's sometimes (hard / hardly)[5] for him to get away from work.

Scene 4: In the street

Mrs A: Have you heard the (terrible / terribly)[1] news? It is so (sad / sadly)[2].

Mrs B: Yes, it happened this morning. I'm (angry / angrily)[3]. No one expected this to happen so (sudden / suddenly)[4].

Mrs B: Mandy was a (beautiful / beautifully)[5] young woman. What a (horrible / horribly)[6] thing to happen.

Scene 5: At work

Colleague 1:   Why did Mandy choose such an (abusive / abusively)[1] partner?

Colleague 2:   I don't know. Why should such a (gentle / gently)[2] person choose such a (nasty / nastily)[3] partner? I think Bill Miller was not at all (kind / kindly)[4] to her.

Colleague 3:   It's really (strange / strangely)[5]. I heard that he treated his first wife very (good / well)[6]. How could this happen to Mandy?

B   Answer the following questions based on the text.

1   How has Mandy's behaviour worried her boss recently?

2   What explanation for her behaviour does Mandy give her boss?

3   What did Mrs A hear and see yesterday?

4   What does Mrs B think about Bill Miller?

5   How does Mandy explain to the counsellor why Bill is often late?

6   What has Mandy already told the counsellor about Bill?

7   What might have happened in the Miller home this morning?

8   What are Mandy's colleagues wondering about?

1 Word power: talking about violence and victimization in schools

A Tick the correct word to complete these collocations for talking about violence and victimization in schools.

1	dysfunctional	☐ harassment	✓ families
2	gang	☐ fights	☐ situation
3	humiliating	☐ pressure	☐ situations
4	messed-up	☐ adults	☐ pressure
5	nasty	☐ behaviour	☐ media
6	peer	☐ families	☐ pressure
7	school	☐ behaviour	☐ violence
8	social	☐ fights	☐ media
9	sexual	☐ adults	☐ harassment
10	thoughtless	☐ behaviour	☐ pressure
11	traditional	☐ violence	☐ bullying

B Complete the text using the collocations you have found above.

Fewer knife fights and very little sexual violence but bullying and harassment still common in Britain's schools

According to a recent survey, _____ _____ [1] at secondary schools in Britain is changing. When schools up and down the country banned knives and other weapons, _____ [2] more or less vanished from the school playground. In most schools, however, almost all other types of _____ _____ [3] are still common.

Teachers reported an increase in cyberbullying, for example, and said that the use of _____ _____ [4] such as Facebook to harass fellow students is widespread. Digital photos showing pupils in _____ [5] are sent around a school by hitting a key. Most of the time, this is seen by the pupils as just having fun but, when the victim is a sensitive person, this kind of _____ [6], can cause a lot of pain.

As one teacher commented, "Cyberbullying is actually a hundred times worse than _____

_____ [7]. Personal emails commenting on someone's figure or photos showing a pupil in a sexy pose, which the kids send around to their friends, can be very hurtful. Pupils save these photos and laugh about them in the playground. There's a lot of _____ [8] involved. If someone doesn't join in the fun, they are likely to be the next victim."

Asked for other reasons for the increases in violence, teachers commented on the way children are treated at home. "Some parents are so busy fighting with each other, taking drugs or drinking heavily that they have no time for their children," one headmaster said. "Children from _____ _____ [9] like these will eventually grow up to be _____ [10] themselves and the patterns will continue into the next generation."

Looking into incidents of sexual abuse in schools, the survey found that pupils often used social media

---

as a way to engage in _____ | most pupils consider rape and other types of sexual
_____[11] and viewed this kind of behaviour, | violence to be serious crimes, and incidents of this
together with other types of cyberbullying | type of physical sexual abuse were rare in schools.
incidents, as "just having a bit of fun". In contrast, | (350 words)

C Do the following tasks based on the text.   > *Umgang mit Operatoren: SB p. 210*

1 Say what the text is about.
2 Point out the result of banning knives and weapons from schools.
3 Describe two examples of cyberbullying.
4 Explain why cyberbullying can be worse than traditional bullying.
5 Explain the reason why violence and victimization in schools is likely to continue.
6 Contrast the two types of sexual abuse considered in the survey.

---

2 **Suggesting solutions to problems**   > *If-sentences: SB p. 230*

You would like to give the parents of some victimized school children advice. Read the situations, then rewrite
sentences a and b by putting the verbs into the correct form to make type 1 *if*-sentences.

1 Fiona used to be very active in school until she was harassed by her classmates.

   a If you (talk) to Fiona's class teacher about the problem, the victimization (stop).

   _____

   b (Fiona / probably take up) her activities again if the victimization (stop).

   _____

2 This parent's daughter doesn't want to go to school because she says the teacher doesn't like people from her
   country.

   a If you (tell) the headmaster about the teacher, (she / get into trouble) with the school board.

   _____

   b The headmaster (make a complaint) if he (believe) the teacher is racist.

   _____

3 This parent's daughter has stopped eating.

   a If your daughter (be willing) to get treatment, you (find) helpline numbers in the phone book.

   _____

   b Your family doctor (refer) you to a family counsellor if your daughter (not want) to have treatment.

   _____

4 This parent's son was a victim of gang violence. The boy has stopped going to school.

   a If your son (be) unhappy at his current school, he (never want) to go back there.

   _____

   b Your son (be) happier if you (transfer) him to a different school.

   _____

C I'm listening

1

Word power: telephone counselling

Complete the mind map with phrases from the box.

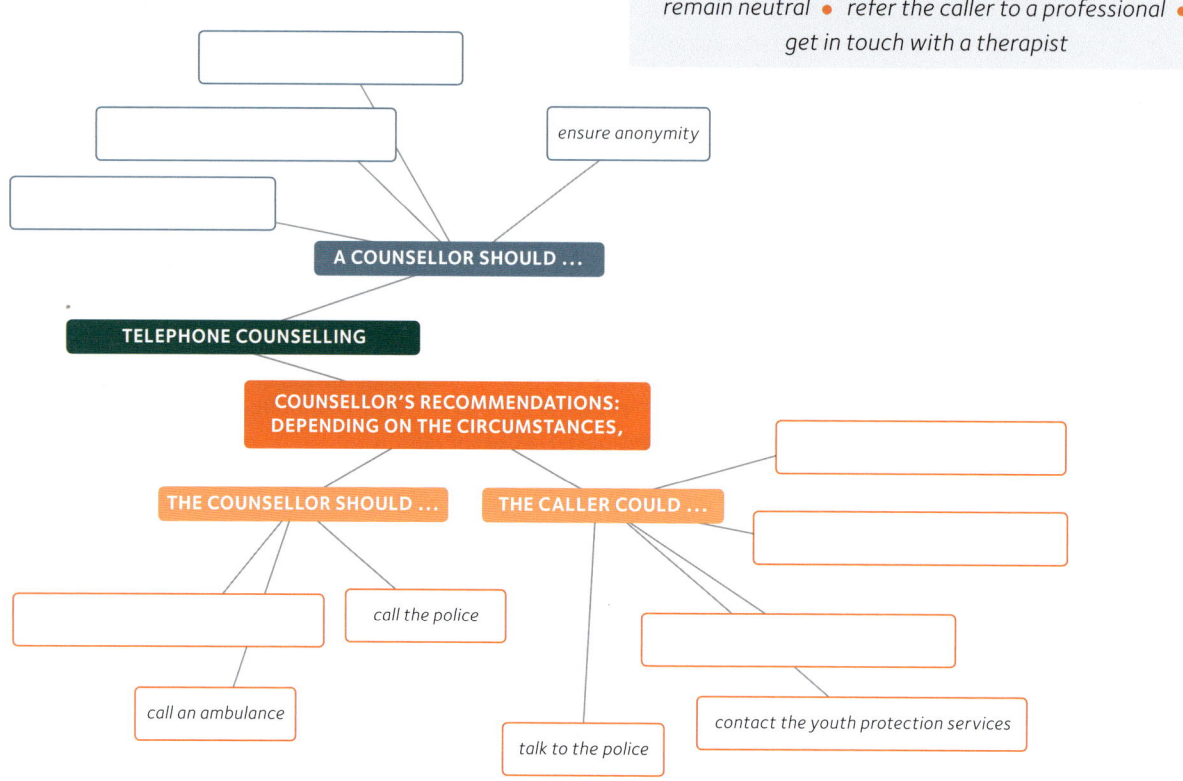

contact Alcoholics Anonymous • talk to a doctor • remain non-judgemental • use silence • remain neutral • refer the caller to a professional • get in touch with a therapist

ensure anonymity

A COUNSELLOR SHOULD …

TELEPHONE COUNSELLING

COUNSELLOR'S RECOMMENDATIONS: DEPENDING ON THE CIRCUMSTANCES,

THE COUNSELLOR SHOULD …

THE CALLER COULD …

call the police

call an ambulance

talk to the police

contact the youth protection services

2

Tips for active listening

Complete the sentences with words from the box to make tips for active listening.

encourage • face-to-face • focussed • judge • open • problem • repeat • respect • silence • sounds • summarize • time • trust • understand

- If you use appropriate words and make _____¹ like "uh-huh", "mmm, mmm", then the caller will know you are listening and that you _____².

- You can _____³ the caller to say more if you _____⁴ some of their own words to them. You can also use your own words to _____⁵ what the caller has just told you.

- Always give the caller _____⁶ to find out what they want to say. The caller will use your periods of _____⁷ to think about how to go on.

- If you are _____⁸ on the caller and listen carefully, you will be able to _____⁹ exactly when to ask questions to help the caller to explain their _____¹⁰.

- In a _____¹¹ situation, you should always use _____¹² and unthreatening body language. Nod your head to show that you are listening.

- Never forget that every caller will _____¹³ you with very private information. You should always treat your callers with _____¹⁴ and indicate that you are there to help them.

3

Listening: a telephone counselling session   > *Mit Hörverstehensaufgaben umgehen: SB p. 215*

A You are going to hear a helpline call between a suicide helpline counsellor and a distressed teenager. Read the statements below, then listen and choose the most suitable endings to complete the statements.

1 Der Anrufer meldet sich beim telefonischen Beratungsdienst für selbstmordgefährdete Personen, weil sein bester Freund
   a gestorben ist.
   b darüber nachdenkt, Selbstmord zu begehen.
   c bei einem Autounfall verletzt wurde und vielleicht stirbt.

2 Der Anrufer fühlt sich schuldig, weil er
   a betrunken Auto gefahren ist.
   b seinen Freund zum Fahren überredete.
   c seinen Freund umbrachte.

3 Die Freunde, mit denen der Anrufer in der Schule viel Zeit verbringt,
   a sind alle beliebter als er selbst.
   b sprechen mit ihm über seinen Freund.
   c hassen den Anrufer.

4 Der Anrufer hat schon einmal
   a darüber nachgedacht, Selbstmord zu begehen.
   b versucht, sich das Leben zu nehmen.
   c das Auto seines Vaters gegen einen Baum gefahren.

5 Der Anrufer sagt, dass er
   a gerade in therapeutischer Behandlung ist.
   b vor einigen Jahren einen Therapeuten konsultierte.
   c niemals zu einem Therapeuten gehen würde.

6 Der Anrufer wird
   a darüber nachdenken, einen Termin mit einem Therapeuten auszumachen.
   b die Telefonnummer eines Therapeuten heraussuchen.
   c einen Therapeuten anrufen.

1	2	3	4	5	6

B Complete the sentences from the counselling session with words from the box. You can listen again to check your answers.

> *alone • apologize • blaming • dealing with • feeling horrible • feelings • in pain •*
> *need some help • suicide • therapist • willing to talk • understand • worried*

1 I _____ that you're _____ about your friend.

2 Can you tell me more about your _____ ?

3 So, you're _____ your friend's accident, and you're also _____ .

4 Are you thinking of committing _____ ?

5 So you're _____ about Spike's death and you're feeling really _____ right now.

6 You think everyone is _____ you for what happened.

7 Would you be _____ to the _____ again?

8 There's no need to _____ . You _____ right now.

7 Cultural contexts

A Freedom of movement

1

Word power : migration and the economy

A Check that you know how to talk about the countries and nationalities by completing the table.

Country	Nationality	Country	Nationality	Country	Nationality
Australia	_____ 1	Italy	_____ 6	Spain	_____ 11
Austria	_____ 2	_____ 7	Dutch	_____ 12	Swiss
_____ 3	Bulgarian	Poland	_____ 8	_____ 13	Turkish
France	_____ 4	Romania	_____ 9	United Kingdom	_____ 14
Greece	_____ 5	Serbia	_____ 10	United States	_____ 15

B Match the two parts of these collocations often used to talk about migration and the economy. They can all be found on page 83 of the Student's book.

1 demographic   a country
2 age   b growth
3 migrant   c group
4 positive   d influence
5 fresh   e approach
6 international   f distribution
7 economic   g trade
8 host   h background

1		2		3		4	
5		6		7		8	

C Translate these phrases into German. You can use a dictionary if you want.

1 to be economically beneficial   _____

2 the availability of labour   _____

3 to relocate production abroad   _____

4 a positive influence on productivity   _____

5 to contribute to cultural diversity   _____

D Complete the following text with expressions from the box.

> demographic issues • labour market • economic growth • local population • skills shortage •
> host country • birth rates • create jobs • ageing population

Migration is influenced by a combination of economic, political and social factors, either in the migrant's country of origin or the _____¹. In the latter, migration can be a tool to solve the problem of _____² on the _____³. In Europe at the moment, one of the most important _____⁴ is deciding how to deal with the problem of an _____⁵. As _____⁶ continue to fall, this is getting worse and will soon have an impact on the _____⁷ of countries like Germany and Sweden. Migrants are also consumers of goods and services which helps _____⁸ rather than taking work away from the _____⁹.

2 **Writing: explaining statistics**

Look at the statistics on population density in Europe. What do they show? What reasons could there be for the differences in population density? How might the figures change in the next five years? Write a description of the chart and answer the questions according to your own opinion. Use the terms in the box to help you.

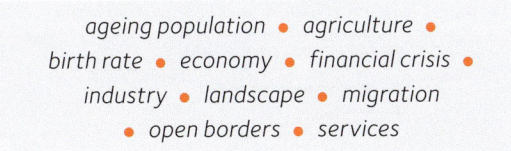

ageing population • agriculture •
birth rate • economy • financial crisis •
industry • landscape • migration
• open borders • services

> *Schaubilder und Statistiken beschreiben*
> *und analysieren: SB p. 218*

Population density in Europe
Number of people per square kilometre

Malta	**1,315.0**
England	402.1
Holland	398.5
Germany	230.0
Italy	199.9
Poland	121.8
Portugal	117.2
France	99.4
Spain	93.5
Romania	89.3
Ireland	67.5
Scotland	67.0
Sweden	21.2
Finland	15.8

nach: House of Commons Library

3 **Comparing information on migration: comparatives and superlatives**

A Complete the statements with the comparative or superlative form of the adjective in brackets.

Mario: I'm sure the unemployment rate is _____¹ (high) in the migrant population.

Lena: I believe that living in a multi-cultural environment makes people _____² (tolerant).

Sylvia: Migration certainly makes a country _____³ (colourful) but it may mean _____⁴ (few) jobs for locals.

Mick: Migration is the _____⁵ (effective) way to ensure economic growth continues.

Anna: In my opinion, new migrants are _____⁶ (unwilling) than in the past to adapt to the way of life in this country.

Martin: The _____⁷ (positive) effect of migration is that it helps

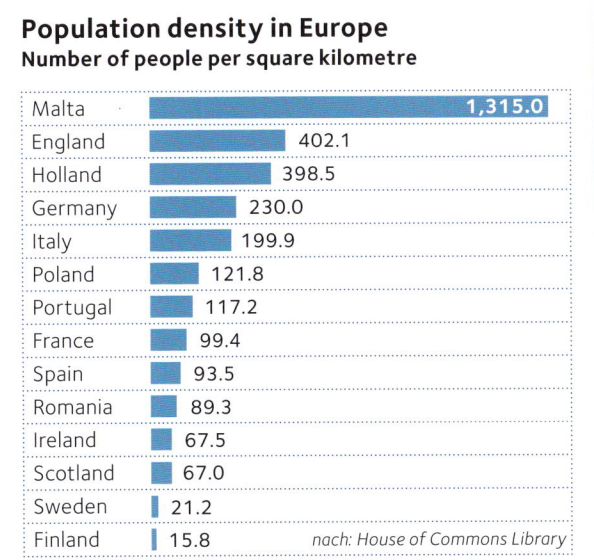

our economy to grow and its _____⁸ (negative) effect is that we are losing our national culture.

> *Comparison of adjectives and adverbs: SB p. 233*

B The speakers in exercise 2A have different opinions. Read what they say again and answer the questions.

1 Who seems in favour of migration? _____

2 Who seems opposed to migration? _____

3 Who seems undecided? _____

B Intercultural encounters

1 **Word power: the migrant experience**

A People migrate for a variety of reasons. Complete the statements with expressions from the box.

economic situation • globetrotter • good reputation • lifestyle • refugee camp • risk-taker

IT specialists from India have a very _____¹ here so it was quite easy to get a good job.

I'm not really a _____² so I chose somewhere not so far from home. There are plenty of jobs in Sweden and I definitely plan to stay for a few more years.

We had to leave Syria because of the war. Our life in a _____³ is terrible but it's our only chance.

You'd probably call me a _____⁴! I've worked in Japan for a while now and I'm off to Mexico next month.

When we retired, we decided to change our _____⁵ completely. We'd been to Thailand on holiday a few times and had got to love the place.

We came to Germany because of the _____⁶ at home. We like it here, but want to return home once the situation improves.

B Migrants hope to improve their lives in various ways. Complete this sentence for each of the speakers in exercise 1A using the most suitable expression from the box.

better career opportunities	better quality of life	more exciting lifestyle
healthier environment	higher salary	lower cost of living
more interesting job	safer environment	warmer weather

 Now I/we have … because …

2 **Reading: reasons for relocating**

A Complete the text about Annika Müller with the sentence parts in the box.

because of the high level of unemployment there	worked in another field for over three years
rather than remaining unemployed at home	I can easily come home at weekends
emigrating forever has gone out of fashion	I've decided to search elsewhere

Annika Müller is looking for a job and she doesn't mind where it is. Along with many others, she's come to an

information event about career opportunities in Denmark at her local employment office in Düsseldorf.

Annika has been unemployed for over six months. After she left school she did a traineeship at a bank but then

_____¹ because her employer couldn't keep her on

after her training. Because she hasn't found a job yet, she wants to try outside Germany and thinks Denmark

could be the solution. Initially, she wanted to go to Spain because she speaks Spanish pretty well but

_____², she gave up that idea.

"There's nothing keeping me in Germany so _____³. Salaries in Scandinavia are usually higher and I've heard that working conditions there are very good. Denmark is not so far from my home town so _____ [4] if I feel like it. I've already checked the prices of flights."

Studies conducted by government institutes show that many young Germans are leaving the country every year, but just as many come back. The trend seems to be for people to work abroad for a few years, return home, then possibly go off again for another few years. The data suggests that _____ _____ [5].

Gathering international experience is also an advantage when people return to Germany. Many German employers place a lot of importance on foreign language skills and cultural competence and welcome employees who have shown the initiative to work abroad _____ [6].

Annika has already started learning Danish and has booked a weekend trip to Copenhagen to try out her language skills.

B Highlight the parts of the text which give you the following information.

1   Four reasons why Annika wants to find work abroad / in Denmark.
2   Ways in which you gain from working abroad.
3   Three things Annika has done to help her reach her goal.

---

3 **Describing past experiences: a cross-cultural anecdote**

A Complete the following anecdote of a cross-cultural encounter of a group of French students with the correct form of the verbs in the box.

> arrive • come • decide • find • get • come • wait • go • happen • hear •
> leave • sit • start • take • talk • wait

A group of French students _____ just _____ [1] in Brighton for an exchange programme. On the first evening they _____ [2] to go to a pub. They _____ [3] so much about British pubs and there are plenty of them in Brighton. They soon _____ [4] a nice one and _____ [5] in and _____ [6] down. They _____ [7] a lot and _____ [8] much notice of what _____ [9] around them but after a while they _____ [10] to wonder why no one _____ [11] to take their order. They _____ [12] and _____ [13], but nobody _____ [14]. After another half an hour, they _____ [15] pretty angry and _____ [16] the pub.

> Past tenses: SB p. 223

B What do you think went wrong?

_____

_____

C Setting down in a new country

Word power: nouns and verbs

Complete the table. You can use a dictionary if you want.

noun	verb
increase	_____ 1
_____ 2	employ
_____ 3	compare
_____ 4	integrate

noun	verb
_____ 5	immigrate
_____ 6	explain
education	_____ 7
_____ 8	organize

2

Word power: talking about young immigrants

A Combine one word from the box with one word below to make collocations you can use to talk about young immigrants at school in Germany. The collocations are all on page 86 of the Student's Book.

> burden • classes • college • instruction • language •
> learner • ~~numbers~~ • rise • staff • system

1 large *numbers* _____

2 sharp _____

3 huge _____

4 education _____

5 regular _____

6 qualified _____

7 second _____

8 language _____

9 fast _____

10 technical _____

B Use the collocations you found above to complete the text.

Because of the _____ 1 in the number of immigrants to Germany in

2012, many schools had to cope with pupils who could not speak German. The German _____

_____ 2 was suddenly faced with a _____ 3: where to find and

finance enough _____ 4 to teach German as a _____

_____ 5 to such _____ 6 of pupils. In some

parts of Germany, volunteers supported the schools so that teachers had more time to give immigrant

pupils extra _____ 7. The pupils were glad to attend the special

classes, and the _____ 8 were quickly integrated into _____

_____ 9. Some of the pupils would like to study at a German university or _____

_____ 10.

3

7

Listening: coping with problems

> *Mit Hörverständnisaufgaben umgehen: SB p. 215*

Listen to the recording and choose the best ending to complete the German sentences.

1   Als Adam gerade nach Deutschland gekommen
    war,
    a   mochte er es, anders zu sein.
    b   genierte er sich wegen seiner Hautfarbe.
    c   bat er seine Mitmenschen, ihn in Ruhe zu
        lassen.

2   Adam mag es nun, zur Schule zu gehen, weil er
    a   sich in eine somalische Schülerin verliebt hat.
    b   sich daran gewöhnt hat.
    c   andere Schüler aus seiner Heimat kennt.

3   Als Lee in Deutschland eintraf,
    a   fühlte er sich anders als die anderen Schüler.
    b   hatte er kein Geld.
    c   fühlte er sich kalt.

4   Lees Leben wurde besser, als er
    a   mit dem Longboarden begann.
    b   seinen Kleidungsstil änderte.
    c   Läden fand, in denen er die Art Kleidung kaufen
        kann, die er mag.

5   Als Rosa nach Deutschland kam,
    a   konnte sie keinen Freund finden.
    b   hatte sie Schwierigkeiten, Freundschaften zu
        knüpfen.
    c   hatte sie nur Freundinnen.

6   Rosa ist nun glücklicher, weil sie
    a   viele Freunde und Freundinnen hat.
    b   weiß, wie sie für ihre Rechte zu kämpfen hat.
    c   die Schulregeln respektiert.

7   Nikita war unglücklich in der Schule, weil
    a   sein Vater gestorben war.
    b   er ignoriert wurde.
    c   ihn die anderen Jungen hänselten.

8   In der Schule
    a   achtet er nun nicht darauf, was andere sagen.
    b   gefallen ihm nun die Unterrichtsstunden.
    c   sagt er nun den anderen Kindern, dass sie ruhig
        sein sollen.

1		2		3		4		5		6		7		8	

4

Simple past or past progressive: talking about living in another country

Complete these sentences about moving to another country with the correct form of the verb in brackets.

Before I moved from Poland to England, I attended the 9th grade at school. On arrival in England, I _____[1]

(feel) very unsure of what lay ahead but my mother _____[2] (say) I was worrying too much and that it

would all be OK.

On my first day I _____[3] (understand) nothing. At school they _____[4] (put) me in a class

with a lot of other immigrants.

While I was learning English, I made a lot of new friends, not just from England but from other parts of Europe.

I quickly _____[5] (pick) up the language and even _____[6] (dream) in English.

However, the problem _____[7] (start) when I _____[8] (phone) my grandmother back in

Poland the first time. I _____[9] (not notice) that I _____[10] (speak) to her in English until

she _____[11] (tell) me. I _____[12] (realize) that slowly I _____[13] (lose) the ability

to speak Polish! So in the summer holidays I _____[14] (go) back to Poland for six weeks and while I

_____[15] (stay) with my grandmother I only spoke Polish.

A Great place to work

1 Word power: an introduction to Human Resources Management

A Complete the text on Human Resources Management with four expressions from the box. You can also find the expressions on page 94 of the Student's Book.

> career development • diversity management • employee engagement • health and safety •
> recruitment • performance appraisal • staff retention • staff welfare

Human Resource managers deal with different issues affecting the people working in an organization. This involves the _____¹ of new staff with the skills the company needs as well as supporting the existing staff. For example, good HRM encourages _____² by making sure the working conditions motivate the staff to contribute to achieving the goals of the company. Having a motivated workforce is the first step to a high level of _____³. This is important for the smooth running of a company because fluctuation of staff means increased costs. Another way to enhance staff productivity is to offer trainings. Trainings are the best way to support staff in their _____⁴ and increase their loyalty to the firm.

B Look at the list of issues HR professionals have to deal with and define them in your own words. Use a dictionary if necessary.

Term	Definition	
absenteeism		1
arbitrator		2
benefit		3
career path		4
exit interview		5
job sharing		6
performance-related bonus		7
remote working		8

C Translate the terms in exercise 1B into German.

2 Gerunds and infinitives: talking about working conditions

A Complete the following work-related comments with the correct form of the verbs in brackets.

> I don't mind _____¹ (get up) early so I choose _____² (work) flexitime.

> I regret _____³ (move) to the Sales Department because it meant _____⁴ (give up) my desk job.

> My previous employer refused _____⁵ (pay) us for doing overtime so a lot of us stopped _____⁶ (work) there.

Our feedback system enables us all _____ 7 (perform) better and avoid _____ 8 (make) the same mistakes again and again.

I decided to start _____ 9 (work) remotely last year and immediately missed _____ 10 (see) my colleagues every morning.

B Complete these sentences about your career plans in your own words.   > *Gerund/Infinitive: SB p. 231*

1 When I finish school, I'm planning _____

2 I'm considering _____

3 I wouldn't mind _____

---

3 **Reading: innovative workspaces**

A Read the interview about the importance of innovative working environments and put the questions below in the correct order.

a   So what's the best workplace design for encouraging creativity in your opinion?
b   Just how funky and cool does a workspace have to be to inspire innovative thinking?
c   How important is it for companies to be innovative anyway?
d   What is the most important design principle companies should consider?

☐
Looking at leading companies like Google and Apple, it seems that every creative organization must promise its staff free food, slides, scooters and areas for chilling and playing table soccer. On the other hand, on a tour of a very successful US company recently, the games area was pointed out to me as the place you spend time in if you want to get fired! So you see, opinions vary.

☐
From the example I just mentioned, we can see that there isn't a magic recipe for designing a workplace which is going to be right for everyone – and right for every company. It's not enough to design a workspace which works for you, the design has to be flexible enough to work for other people in your company, too.

☐
Well, as I said, flexibility is extremely important. The idea that individuals working in closed rooms come up with brilliantly creative ideas is out-dated. The best ideas come when people share their insights so there must be open project areas for this purpose. Private spaces for intensive discussions without interruption are a must, too. And, there should be a café-like area for informal talk, where teams from different projects and departments can mix and exchange ideas.

☐
It's vital. I think nearly everyone would agree that innovation is what allows companies to grow. They need staff who see new opportunities and are able to put them into practice. It's not enough to only improve existing products, innovation means coming up with something which didn't exist before.

B Find expressions in the interview that have the same meaning as the following German expressions.

1 *etwas in die Tat umsetzen:* _____

2 *auf etwas hinweisen:* _____

3 *es reicht nicht:* _____

4 *etwas wachsen lassen:* _____

> *Schwierige Texte lesen: SB p. 210*
> *Mit unbekannten Wörtern umgehen: SB p. 210*

B Working conditions in Europe and beyond

1 **Word power: global labour market**

A How many collocations can you form using the words in the boxes? Use one word from each box. Sometimes more than one match is possible.

> working • job • much-needed • diverse •
> critical • skilled • ageing

> hours • conditions • time • seekers •
> security • skills • workforce

B Use the collocations you found in exercise 1A to translate these German expressions. All the expressions can also be found on pages 96 and 97 of the Student's Book.

1 *berufliche Fertigkeiten* _____

2 *alternde Arbeitnehmerschaft* _____

3 *Arbeitsbedingungen* _____

4 *entscheidende Fähigkeiten* _____

5 *Arbeitssuchende(r)* _____

6 *Fachpersonal* _____

7 *Arbeitszeit* _____

8 *Arbeitsplatzsicherheit* _____

C Complete the sentences with the correct preposition.

1 A divide is developing _____**between**_____ the industrialized countries and the developing world.

2 Businesses have to adapt _____ changing needs.

3 In spite _____ better educational opportunities, many young people are unemployed.

4 Companies must accept that they have to invest more _____ staff training.

5 The skills shortage means that employers are taking _____ more female and older staff.

6 Increased demand for skills in new technology is an advantage _____ young people.

2 **Analysing statistical data**

A Look at the three graphs showing the age structure of the German population in 1950, 2000 and 2050. Describe and analyse the information.

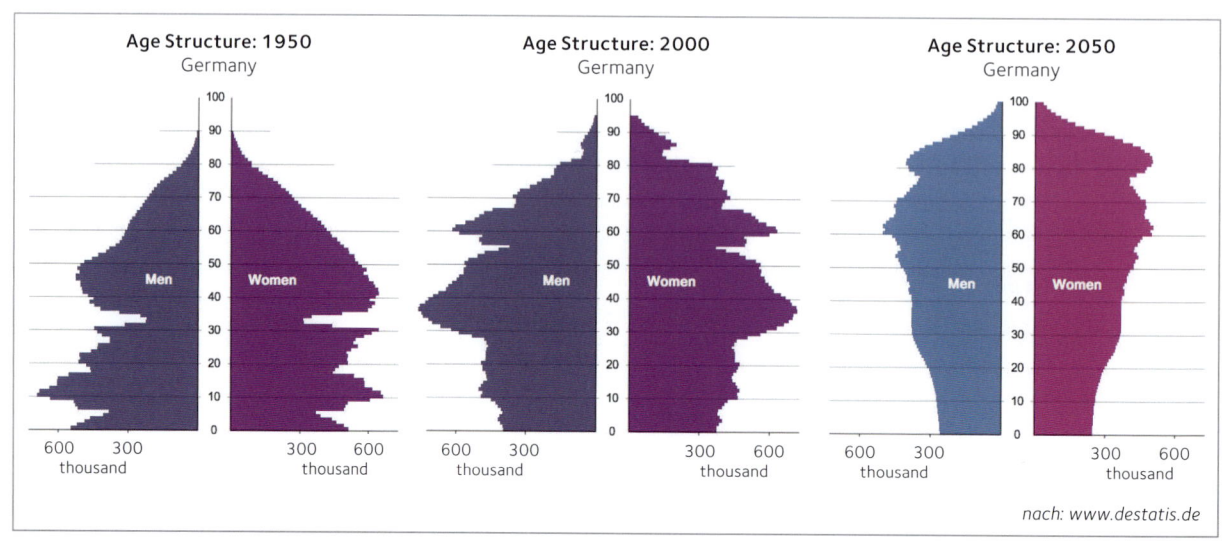

nach: www.destatis.de

B Think about the impact that the demographic development shown in the graphs will have on the labour market in Germany. Write a short text expressing your opinion.

> *Schaubilder und Statistiken beschreiben und analysieren: SB p. 218*
> *Textproduktion: Umgang mit Operatoren: SB p. 210*

3 **Reading: young people in the workforce**

A Read the following blog post on the problems young people have in the working world. While you read, make brief notes on the issues the blogger mentions in the table below. Do you agree or disagree? Why?

◀ ▶ + www.digitaljoy.blogs.com

| ABOUT | PRODUCTS | BLOG | PRESS | CONTACT | DIGITAL JOY! |

10 October 20.. | Young & digital

More and more employers find that the young people they hire are not able to interact confidently. They seem to have problems working effectively in teams with colleagues and developing relationships with clients. Employers see one basic reason for this: young workers would rather send an instant message than walk over to speak directly to a colleague. They spend hours texting and playing games on smartphones, but consider speaking to someone on the phone a waste of time. They contact their friends via social networks instead of chatting over coffee. More often than not, for them socializing or taking part in group activities means meeting online rather than in person. Because they rely so much on online communication, young employees lack experience in face-to-face interaction and have not learned how to speak clearly and concisely, listen carefully and read other people's expressions and body language.

36 comments

Issues mentioned in the blog	agree/disagree	Reasons for my opinion
Main problem		
Reasons and/or results		

> *Schwierige Texte lesen: SB p. 210*

B Complete these sentences from the blog post with your own opinion about young people today. Use the same form (i.e. gerund or infinitive) as is used in the blog.

1 Young workers would rather *use a keyboard than write with a pen.* _____

2 They spend hours _____

3 They consider _____

4 Socializing means _____

5 They have not learned _____

> *Gerund/Infinitive: SB p. 231*

C When things go wrong

1 **Word power: working environment**

A The terms and phrases in the box below are all connected to job satisfaction. For each term or phrase decide whether it is positive, negative or both in your opinion.

benefits • bullying • burnout • disputes • financial incentives • insecurity • labour leasing • parental leave • pay rise • performance appraisal • remote working • restructuring

positive	negative	positive or negative

B Choose two terms or phrases you think can be seen as both positive and negative and explain the two sides of these issues.

1 _____

_____

2 _____

_____

2 **Listening: job dissatisfaction**

8

A Read the top 10 reasons for job dissatisfaction below. Then listen to three people talking about their work situation and decide which reason given in the list each speaker is talking about. Listen again and note down the words and expressions which tell you which reason they are referring to.

These are the top ten reasons employees gave for being unhappy at their work:

#1	My boss is a bad manager so the working atmosphere is not good.	#6	I have no hope of getting any promotion.
#2	I no longer have any interest in my work.	#7	I worry a lot about being laid off.
#3	My work is not challenging enough so I have no chance of personal development.	#8	I don't get enough praise or recognition from my boss.
#4	There are far too many rules so there is no chance of taking responsibility.	#9	I feel a lack of identification with the values of my company.
#5	The salaries at the company are too low. Most people feel underpaid.	#10	The grass looks greener in other companies. They are offering better benefits.

1 _____

_____

2 _____

_____

3 _____

_____

B The three speakers use examples of idiomatic language. What do these expressions mean?

> *My career has hit a brick wall.* [1]

> *It's a sink or swim environment.* [2]

> *Most of my tasks are no-brainers.* [3]

> *Mit Hör-/Sehverstehensaufgaben umgehen: SB p. 215*

3 Communication skills: on the phone

A Match the following questions to the responses.

1. Would you like me to check that for you?
2. Can you speak up a bit, please? I can't hear you.
3. Would you like to call back later?
4. Would you like to leave a message for her?
5. I'm sorry, what was the name again, please?

a. It's Mara Simon from the HR department.
b. Yes, please. Could you tell her that I'll be a bit late for our appointment tomorrow?
c. I'll be in a meeting then so I'll just send an email instead.
d. I'm already shouting. The line is very bad.
e. That would be great, please do. I need the information rather urgently.

1	2	3	4	5

B Read the transcript of a telephone call in which both speakers do a very bad job. How would you improve it? Make up any details.

> *Telephoning: SB p. 203*

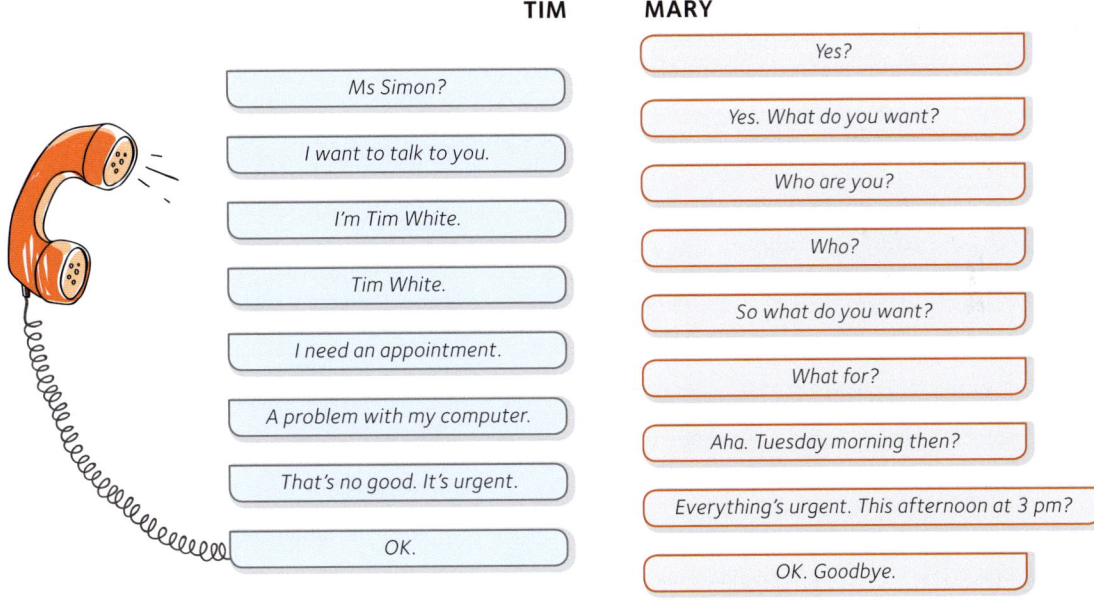

TIM

- Ms Simon?
- I want to talk to you.
- I'm Tim White.
- Tim White.
- I need an appointment.
- A problem with my computer.
- That's no good. It's urgent.
- OK.

MARY

- Yes?
- Yes. What do you want?
- Who are you?
- Who?
- So what do you want?
- What for?
- Aha. Tuesday morning then?
- Everything's urgent. This afternoon at 3 pm?
- OK. Goodbye.

4 Word power: workplace disputes

What behaviour on the part of colleagues or employers lead to disputes at work? Find five examples in the word snake.

ANFWITHOLDINGINFORMATIONRETOIGNORINGSUGGESTIONSMALTREFUSINGSALARYINCREASESPAREUNDERSTAFFINGDEPARTMENTSREFFIOVERCROWDINGOFFICESPACEPOWD

A Winners and losers of globalization

1 **Word power: the effects of globalization**

A Match the words in the box to the words in the list to form collocations useful when talking about the effects of globalization.

> affordable • assembly • container • low-wage • job • manufacturing • non-governmental •
> offshore • semi-finished • short-term • trade • win-win

1 _____ barriers

2 _____ contracts

3 _____ costs

4 _____ countries

5 _____ goods

6 _____ line

7 _____ opportunities

8 _____ organizations

9 _____ prices

10 _____ production

11 _____ shipping

12 _____ situation

B Complete the three texts using the expressions you found in 1A. Then match the titles a–c to the texts.

a How globalization affects consumers

b The effects of globalization on companies

c Are employees the losers of globalization?

☐

The purpose of _____¹ is to lower costs. This is the reason that companies are always looking for suppliers who offer the lowest prices. The bad working conditions at the _____² in Asia are a direct result of this. Although _____³ try hard to protect workers' rights, the conditions rarely improve. Even in their home countries, companies have to stay competitive by lowering costs and increasing flexibility. They achieve this by offering more and more part-time jobs and _____⁴.

1

☐

Globalization has its advantages, too. Products from all over the world are now available at _____⁵ because transport costs have fallen dramatically due to the growth of _____⁶. Additionally, _____⁷ are kept at a minimum because of global competition. These savings can then be passed on to the consumer. Poorer countries benefit from globalization mainly because it provides better _____⁸.

2

☐

Globalization means that a company's competitors are all over the world. _____⁹ have broken down and the production of goods often takes place in _____¹⁰. Both of these factors enable companies to lower their costs. Additionally, companies can decide whether they need suppliers of raw materials or of _____¹¹. It's a _____¹² for both the companies and the suppliers.

3

2   Reading: cost structure of a bar of chocolate

A   When a bar of chocolate is sold, cocoa farmers, manufacturing companies, exporters/local traders and retailers all earn a certain share of the price. Read the text and complete the pie chart.

The true cost of a bar of chocolate

When a consumer goes into a shop and buys a bar of chocolate, the retailer's share of the sale price is 17%. But who gets the remaining 83%?

Chocolate manufacturing is big business with net sales worth about 88 billion dollars in 2014. Ten multi-national companies dominate the market, compete for market share and make high profits. 70% of the world's cocoa is grown in Africa and the millions of cocoa farmers there get a smaller and smaller share of the revenues – many of them end up earning no more than $2 a day. Most of the money is made once the cocoa beans have reached the cocoa and chocolate manufacturing companies. When a consumer buys a bar of chocolate, these companies receive 70% of the retail price. The cocoa farmers' share is a mere 6%. In the 1980s, the respective figures were 58% and 16%.

90% of the world's cocoa is grown on small farms. Unfortunately, the farmers are not organized and have little knowledge of the market prices. Therefore, local traders act as middlemen between the farmers and the exporters. The local traders, however, pay the farmers far less than the international market price to compensate for the high government taxes they themselves have to pay. The farmers are powerless.

The market price for cocoa goes up and down as supply and demand varies. These variations can be a result of extreme weather, financial speculation or political instability in the producing countries. Cocoa exporters try to balance these variations by storing beans and regulating the amount sold to the cocoa and chocolate manufacturers. Together with the local traders, their share of the final price is around 7%.

(279 words)

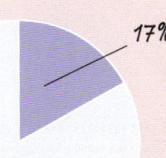

17% retailer

B   What do the following figures from the text refer to?
1 58%   2 70%   3 $2   4 90%   5 83%

> *Schwierige Texte lesen: SB p. 210*

3   Listening: the growth of globalization

9

A   There are many reasons for globalization. Listen to part of a talk on its causes and underline the issues in the box that are referred to. Note that you will not hear the exact words.

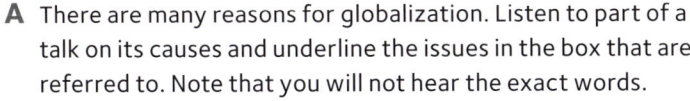

container shipping • communication technology • e-commerce • economies of scale • mass media • mobility of labour • multi-national companies • NGOs • popular culture • trade barriers

B   Listen again and find expressions in the talk which mean the same as the following.

1   for many reasons: _____

2   can benefit from: _____

3   been closely associated with: _____

4   has an impact on: _____

> *Mit Hör-/Sehverstehensaufgaben umgehen: SB p. 215*

1 **Word power: the globalized garment industry**

A Complete the sentences on the production process of a garment by adding the correct form of the verb in brackets.

1 The garments are _____ (sew) in Asia.

2 The garments are exported and _____ (sell) in famous retail chains.

3 Each season's new collection is _____ (design) at our head office.

4 Cotton is _____ (grow) in the USA.

5 The fabric is _____ (cut) by hand.

6 Cotton yarn is _____ (weave) into fabric on hi-tech machines.

B Bring the steps of the production process into the correct order.

| 1 | | 2 | | 3 | | 4 | | 5 | | 6 | |

2 **Writing: the life cycle of a T-shirt**

A Translate the following words into German. You can use a dictionary if you want.

1 clothes recycling bin: _____

2 to grow: _____

3 cotton: _____

4 retail chain: _____

5 to export: _____

6 piece of clothing: _____

7 to sew: _____

8 to donate: _____

9 fabric: _____

10 textile mill: _____

11 to process: _____

13 consumer: _____

12 to weave: _____

14 charity: _____

B Write a short text in English describing the life cycle of a T-shirt using the terms from 2A. You may add any details you like, but try to use as many terms as you can.

3 **The passive: describing a supply chain**

Complete the text with the correct passive form of the verb in brackets.

40,000 miles around the world

"Wash inside out separately / 100% cotton" _____[1] (print) on the inside label of your new pair of jeans. There's no "Made in …" information because which country could _____[2] (mention) there? Your jeans _____[3] (make) not in one but in many countries and have travelled about 40,000 miles around the world by the time you buy them.

The cotton for denim jeans _____ 4 (grow) in Benin, West Africa, and then

_____ 5 (export) to Milan in Italy to _____ 6 (process) and

_____ 7 (weave) into fabric. After that, the fabric _____ 8

(send) back south to Tunisia. There it _____ 9 (cut) and _____ 10

(sew) using polyester thread which may _____ 11 (make) in Northern Ireland, Hungary

or Turkey. The polyester fibre for this thread _____ 12 (manufacture) from oil in Japan.

Zips and buttons are also made in Japan using metal from Namibia or Australia.

> *The passive: SB p. 229*

Listening: changing suppliers

A Listen to the fashion buyers at Z&P discussing a change of suppliers and underline the expression you hear.

1 take account of that / take that into account
2 at the shops / in the shops
3 look for a new supplier / look at a new supplier
4 apart from that / a part of that
5 get to the point / that's the point
6 a new range of products / a new age of products
7 with great detail / in great detail
8 as far as I know / so far as I know
9 allow a profit margin / a lower profit margin
10 any other option / another option

B Listen again and decide whether these statements are true or false. Explain your answers.

		True	False
1	Raffaele doesn't want to discuss fair trade.		
2	Productivity is not as high in China as in Bangladesh.		
3	The company is losing customers.		
4	Ellen is late for the meeting.		
5	Bangladesh's currency is the taka.		

C Write a short summary of the meeting in your own words.

D Certain collocations are often used to talk about the strengths and weaknesses of different supplier countries. Which adjective is the odd one out in the following?

1 high • increased • profit • improved   productivity
2 environmental • safety • high • life   standards
3 increasing • raw • cost • global   inflation
4 fast • new • state-of-the-art • information   technology
5 strong • fluctuating • weak • margin   currency

> *Mit Hör-/Sehverstehensaufgaben umgehen: SB p. 215*
> *Einen Text zusammenfassen: SB p. 216*

C Fair trade

1 **Word power**

A Put the words from the word cloud into the correct categories in the table. Some words fit into more than one category.

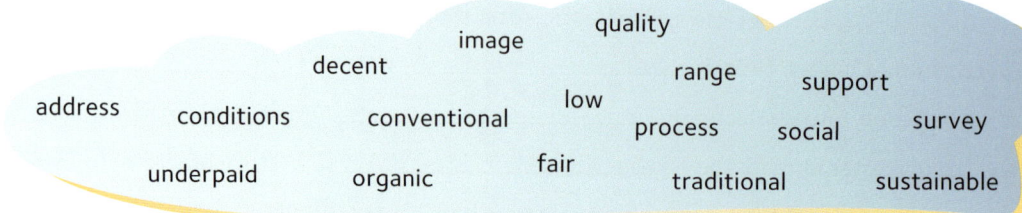

quality
image
range
support
decent
low
address
conditions
conventional
process
social
survey
underpaid
fair
organic
traditional
sustainable

adjective	noun	verb

B Highlight the words in exercise 1A that fit into two categories. Use four of them in the correct form to complete these sentences.

1 The _____ of setting up a fair trade scheme benefits everybody in the long run.

2 The farmers receive a lot of _____ under the fair trade scheme, both financially and socially.

3 The wages in our factory _____ from $4 – $6 a day depending on the job the worker does.

4 Fairtrade is the first organization to _____ the problem of underpaid farmers.

2 **Active or passive: a farmer's view on Fairtrade**

Complete the text about what a farmer says about Fairtrade. Use the correct form of the words in the box.

be able • buy • dictate • earn • fix • guarantee • know • respect • sell

Our crops _____¹ directly to the buyer at a set price, which means that there is no middleman. The

price _____² by Fairtrade and the market no longer _____³ it. Because the price

_____⁴, I now _____⁵ how much money I can _____⁶ and save every month.

For the first time in my life, I _____⁷ to set aside some money for my son's education. When you

_____⁸ a product with a fair trade label, my human rights _____⁹ and my family and I can

lead a better life.

> *The passive: SB p. 229*

3 **Reading and writing: public relations**

A Match the headlines a–c to the sentence excerpts from three newspaper articles. There are two sentences from each article.

a Underpaid and underage

b TO DIE FOR

c FASHION GOING TO WASTE

1	Fashion labels are under fire again for promoting an unhealthy body image to young girls after the death of a top catwalk model.	☐
2	Participating stores donate clothes to NGOs like Oxfam and then buy back the recycled materials for manufacture into new products.	☐
3	Last night's BBC report on the use of child labour in factories under contract to a leading high street fashion store has caused red faces in head office.	☐
4	New advertising campaigns featuring size zero models should be banned according to a government watchdog.	☐
5	More fashion retailers are encouraging customers to bring back unwanted items for recycling as part of the so-called circular economy.	☐
6	This news comes at a very bad time for the company as they have just published disappointing sales figures.	☐

B When a company gets bad publicity, its PR department has to act immediately. Choose one of the topics from exercise 3A and write a short comment on how the company could react to improve its image.

> *Einen Aufsatz oder eine Stellungnahme schreiben: SB p. 216*

4 **Cartoon: Fair trade**

Describe and analyse the cartoon below.
Compare it with the text. Write at least 150 words.

"There was a programme on television last night about organic food which really surprised me. In order to enjoy potatoes throughout the winter, we import them from Egypt. Now, I thought that organic potatoes were grown in soil, but they are actually grown in the desert! Water has to be obtained from underground caves and sprayed down on the crops using huge machines. Most people who buy organic food would be devastated to know that their shopping was so environmentally damaging. And what about the recent trend for retailers to sell organic cotton clothing? These large chains use the same sweatshops they have always used to make the organic cotton clothes. In my opinion that defeats the point completely! A truly ethical business has to think about every single detail involved in the day-to-day running of the organization."

BILL PROUD

'Organic or Fairtrade?'

 **A** A finite planet

1 **Word power: collocations**

A Complete the collocations with verbs from the box.
All of the collocations are in the text on page 118 of the
Student's Book. Then translate them into German.

carry on • come • cut • follow • improve •
meet • pass on • pass on • place • tackle

1 _____ a strain on resources _____

2 _____ one's performance _____

3 _____ one's basic needs _____

4 _____ under pressure _____

5 _____ with business as usual _____

6 _____ profits _____

7 _____ the costs of sth _____

8 _____ problems _____

9 _____ the benefits of sth _____

10 _____ regulations _____

B Use collocations from 1A to complete the sentences.

1 Oil now costs us twice as much as last year: that will _____ by 25% compared to
last year.

2 We will have to _____ to consumers, but that will make us less
competitive.

3 All businesses should _____ about recycling: it would lead to less
pollution.

4 Don't you think we should _____ ourselves rather than leaving them
to future generations?

5 As Earth's population increases, it is certain that more resources will _____
_____ .

6 Continued industrial growth will _____ such as oil and minerals.

7 Some think we will be lucky if we can _____ – never mind about
buying luxury goods.

8 Businesses cannot just _____ and ignore the
problem of dwindling resources.

9 Fortunately many companies are trying to _____ in resource
efficiency.

10 Hopefully they will save on raw materials and energy costs, and _____
to consumers.

2 **Future passive: how will things look in the future?**

Complete the sentences with the future passive of the verbs in brackets.

1   Unless we act now, our climate _____ by CO_2 emissions. (damage)

2   The basic needs of people in developing countries _____ without productivity improvements. (not / meet)

3   Within a few decades, fossil fuels _____ by renewable energy. (replace)

4   Effiency savings _____ to the consumer in the form of lower prices. (pass on)

5   By 2050, coal and gas _____ to produce energy. (not / burn)

6   The energy efficiency of household appliances _____ further. (improve)

7   Will _____? (our demand for luxury goods / satisfy)

8   Soon some of the most important industrial raw materials _____. (use up)

9   How _____? (greater resource efficiency / achieve)

10 Will _____? (solutions to the problem of dwindling resources / find)

> *The passive: SB p. 229*

---

3 **Listening: resource efficiency**

11

Professor Lachlan Mitchell is an expert in resource efficiency. He is talking to a journalist in a radio interview. Listen to their conversation and complete the sentences below with information from the recording.

Oil – a valuable resource to be used efficiently

1   Resource efficiency is a matter of doing as much as we can _____.

2   If you use up the resources that your industry depends upon, you _____.

3   Resource efficiency is a way to invest in _____.

4   It makes sense to use oil carefully, because extracting it _____.

5   Therefore, improving resource efficiency is a way to become _____.

6   Poor resource efficiency wastes money and in the world of business today _____.

7   Demea is a German government agency which was set up to help small and medium-sized companies in Germany to _____.

> *Mit Hör-/Sehverstehensaufgaben umgehen: SB p. 215*

1

Word power: product life cycle

A Complete the mind map with the stages (1–8) in the product life cycle for a laptop.

> assembly • disposal • distribution •
> manufacturing • ~~materials acquisition~~ •
> materials processing • packaging • use

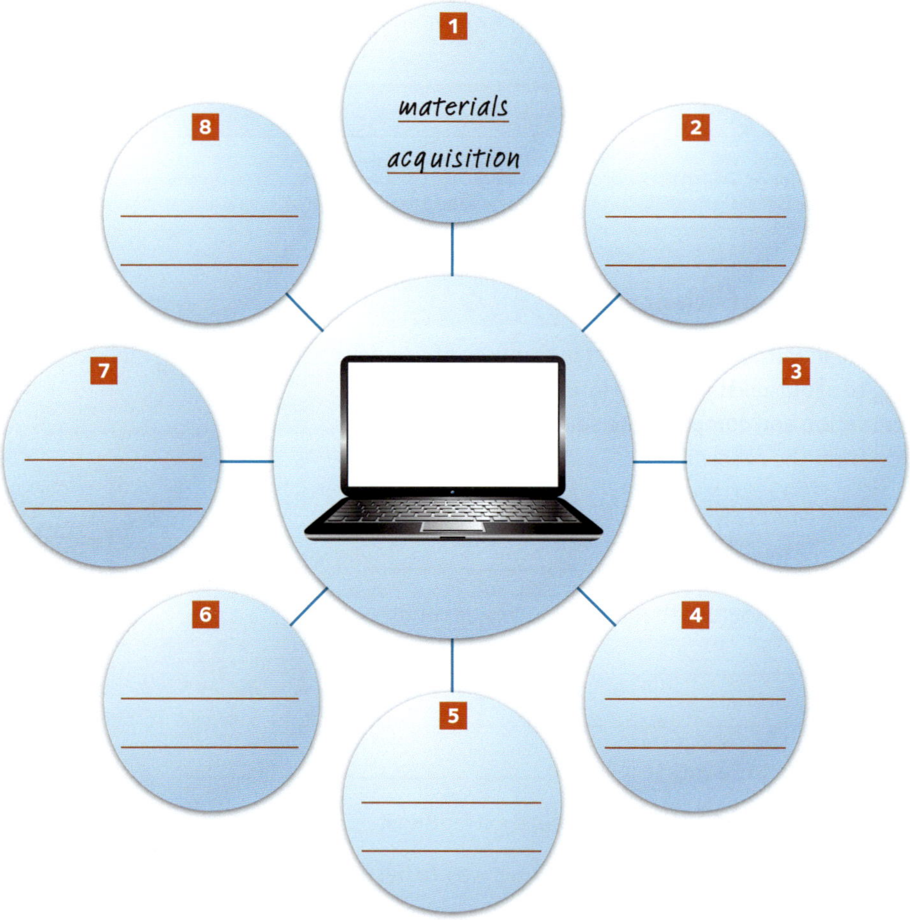

1 materials acquisition

2 _____

3 _____

4 _____

5 _____

6 _____

7 _____

8 _____

B What materials, people, processes, buildings and systems are involved at each stage in the product life cycle? Add them to the mind map. Some may occur more than once.

> *business customers* ● *cardboard* ● *consumers* ● *extraction* ● *factory* ● *finished product* ● *incineration* ●
> *landfill* ● *machining and moulding* ● *metals* ● *oil* ● *ores* ● *plastic granules* ● *plastic film* ● *polystyrene* ●
> *raw materials* ● *recycling* ● *refining* ● *shops* ● *transport networks* ● *warehouses*

C Identify the main environmental impacts that are likely to happen at each stage of the product life cycle and add them to the mind map. Some may occur several times or at every stage.

> CO_2 *emissions* ● *loss of natural habitat* ● *toxic by-products* ● *other pollutants* ● *use of water* ●
> *use of land* ● *use of finite resources*

2
4

Video: Human Impact: Pacific Plastic, Hawaii

A Watch the video and decide which of these descriptions best summarizes its content.

1 Hawaii is still a remote paradise even though there is a problem with plastic debris.
2 The situation on Hawaii's beaches shows that our way of life must change.
3 Plastic is more dangerous to the environment than most people realise.

B Even in the remotest places on Earth, plastic pollution is a problem. Watch the video again and choose the most suitable endings to complete the sentences.

1 Weil die hawaiischen Inseln so fern vom Festland liegen, …

   a ☐ muss man sich auf importierte Güter verlassen.
   b ☐ hat man eine starke Beziehung zum Meer.
   c ☐ wollen viele wegziehen.

2 Die Strände von Hawaii sind stark verschmutzt, weil …

   a ☐ die Insulaner ihren Müll ins Meer werfen.
   b ☐ niemand sich die Mühe gibt, die Strände sauber zu halten.
   c ☐ Ozeansströmungen den Müll anderer Länder Hawaii zutreiben.

3 Von den rund 150 Milliarden Kilo Kunststoff, die jährlich weltweit hergestellt werden …

   a ☐ zersetzt sich die Hälfte schnell in der Umwelt.
   b ☐ wird nur die Hälfte wiederverwertet.
   c ☐ gelangt die Häle in die Umwelt.

4 Wenn Kunststoffmüll auf dem Meer treibt, …

   a ☐ wird es oft in winzige Teilchen zersetzt.
   b ☐ sinkt es nie auf den Meeresgrund.
   c ☐ wird es meistens irgendwo am Strand angeschwemmt.

5 Seevögel …

   a ☐ sterben, wenn sie statt Fischen Kunststoffmüll fressen
   b ☐ können kein Futter finden, weil so viel Kunststoffmüll auf dem Wasser treibt.
   c ☐ fressen nur dann Kunststoff, wenn es sonst nichts zu fressen gibt.

> ❯ *Mit Hör-/Sehverstehensaufgaben umgehen: SB p. 215*

C Greening our business

1

Simple past passive and present perfect passive: improving practices

> *The passive: SB p. 229*

Thanks to a quality management (QM) programme, practices have been improved at the truck factory. Using suitable tenses in the passive, write about how things were done before QM, and how they have been improved since then. Use a *by*-agent where necessary.

	Before QM	Since QM
1	Machining processes use a lot of oil.	Reduce oil use by 50%.
2	Old machines injure several workers.	Install new, safer machines.
3	Inefficient processes waste raw materials.	Improve manufacturing methods.
4	Require frequent service visits.	Cut the number of visits.
5	Allow workers to develop wasteful habits.	Stop bad habits by better training.

1   *Before QM, a lot of oil was used by machining processes.*

    Since QM, _____

2   _____

_____

3   _____

_____

4   _____

_____

5   _____

_____

2

Reading: Precious Plastic

Read the text on page 63 and complete the tasks below. Write one or two sentences per task.

1   Say what the text is about.

_____

_____

2   Explain why Dave undertook this project.

_____

_____

3   Contrast Dave's attitude to that of plastic manufacturing companies.

_____

_____

4   Describe the components of Dave's "plastic factory" and what he can do with them.

_____

_____

5   Explain what "open source" means.

_____

_____

6 Examine why Dave chose to make his project open source.

_____

_____

_____

7 Evaluate whether Dave's project is orginal or uses existing ideas.

_____

_____

_____

_____

> *Umgang mit Operatoren: SB p. 210*

Dave Hakkens' Precious Plastic Factory

Dave Hakkens' Precious Plastic project is a set of simple machines for recycling plastic and making new products locally. He says he got the idea for the project after visiting plastic
5   manufacturing companies and discovering that they were reluctant to use recycled plastic.

"We recycle just 10% [of waste plastic]," says Hakkens.
"I wondered why we recycle so little so I
10   investigated it. I went to all these companies and I realised that they don't really want to use recycled plastic. So I wanted to make my own tools so I could use recycled plastic locally."

The Precious Plastic machines include a plastic shredder [1], an extruder [2], an injection moulder [3] and a rotation moulder [4], which Hakkens made using a combination of new custom-made components and reclaimed parts he found at a scrapyard [5].

15   "I made these machines based on industrial standards," says Hakkens. "But they are all made very simple so you can produce locally. Like a craftsman, you can start working with plastic."

Hakkens designed a range of products to be produced using the machines, including a rotation-moulded waste paper bin [6], an injection-moulded spinning top [7] and an extruded plastic lamp.

However, he says the machines can be used to make a much wider variety of products. "You can make
20   whatever you want," he explains. "Everybody can use [the machines] to make whatever they want and set up their own production."

Precious Plastic is an open-source project and Hakkens hopes other designers will adapt and improve the machines over time. "I developed these machines and I shared them on the internet," Hakkens says. "People can make them on the other side of the world and send some feedback and say, 'Hey, maybe you can do this
25   better'. In the end you'll have this set of machines and you can start a local recycling centre."

(309 words)

¹ Zerkleinerungsmaschine	³ Spritzgießer	⁵ Schrottplatz	⁷ Kreisel
² Strangpresse	⁴ Rotationsformanlage	⁶ Papierkorb	

nach: www.dezeen.com

3   **Translation**

Translate lines 1 to 17 of the text into German.

11 Powering the future

A The right time for solar?

1

Word power: energy

Complete the grid with the English translations of the German words to find an advantage of photovoltaic (PV) systems.

1   The electrical _____ (*Netz*) delivers electricity to homes and businesses.

2   The government has set a _____ (*Ziel*) of cutting CO_2 emissions by 80 per cent.

3   The use of fossil fuels is bad for the _____ (*Umwelt*).

4   As electricity becomes more expensive, households are trying to reduce their _____ (*Verbrauch*).

5   Can the sun and the wind provide all of the _____ (*Energie*) that we need?

6   Our solar panels are 15 years old: maybe it's time to _____ (*modernisieren*) the system.

7   Have you seen this electricity _____ (*Rechnung*)? We have to pay 500 euros!

8   I'm going to find out how much it will cost to _____ (*installieren*) a PV system at home.

9   We couldn't have PV because our home is in the _____ (*Schatten*).

10 The _____ (*Effizienz*) of most solar cells in use today is about 15–19 per cent.

11 Don't delay because of the _____ (*Kosten*) of a PV system: it really doesn't cost that much.

12 On sunny days, households with PV _____ (*speisen*) more electricity into the system than they take from it.

13 Soon it may be possible to have a _____ (*Dach*) made entirely of solar panels.

14 On a sunny day in summer, our solar panels _____ (*generieren*) about 16 kilowatt hours of electricity.

15 Do you think that the _____ (*Versorgungs-*) companies are worried, now that their customers can produce their own electricity?

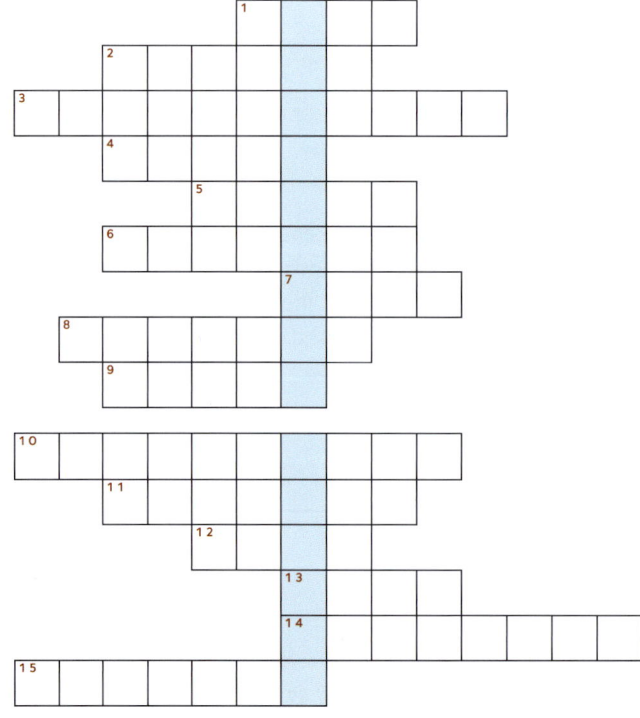

2   **Modal verbs: time to take action**
> *Modal auxiliary verbs: SB p. 226*

Translate the sentences into English using suitable modal verbs.

1   Wir dürfen nicht tatenlos zusehen (*sit back and watch*), während CO2-Emissionen steigen.

2   Wir müssen unseren Verbrauch an fossilen Brennstoffen (*fossil fuel use*) reduzieren.

3   Industrie und Wirtschaft (*the economy*) können auf erneuerbare Energiequellen umsteigen (*switch to*).

4   Das könnte für einige Schwerindustrien (*heavy industries*) schwierig sein.

5   Es muss nicht für die Konjunktur (*state of the economy*) im Allgemeinen schädlich sein.

6   Man sollte sich nicht auf eine einzige Energiequelle verlassen (*rely on*).

7   Wir sollten einen guten Energiemix anstreben (*aim for*).

8   Haushalte können ihren Teil dazu beitragen (*play their part*).

9   Sie könnten auch an einem kommunalen Energieprojekt (*community energy project*) wie z. B. einem Windpark teilnehmen (*take part in*).

3   **Phrases for discussions**

Amy, Ben and Chris are the directors of a small company. They are discussing whether to install solar panels on the roof of their office building. Add the phrases a–j to the dialogue. There is one phrase that you do not need.

a   Sorry, but I don't agree.
b   Yes, that's quite right.
c   The main reason is that
d   Personally, I think that
e   Is everyone happy with that?
f   I don't entirely agree with you.
g   I see what you mean, but
h   Don't you agree?
i   Isn't it fair to say that
j   Yes, I agree.

Amy: ☐ we should install a solar PV system as soon as possible. ☐ we can start saving money now.

Ben: ☐ There's no reason to wait. The longer we wait, the more money we will have paid for electricity. If we install solar panels now – no more electricity bills!

Chris: ☐ The price of solar panels is sinking by 10% every year, so the longer we wait, the cheaper they will be. Also, new solar panels are in development and will be much more efficient than the ones we can buy now.

Amy: ☐ if we took that argument to its logical conclusion, we might never install solar panels at all! We would always be waiting for cheaper solar panels, or new, more efficient solar panel technology.

Ben: Hmm. ☐ we all think the company should install solar panels and that it's just a question of timing?

Chris: ☐ I agree that we should install solar, but now is not the right time. It's a big investment and we don't want to make the wrong choice.

Ben: In that case, I suggest that we set a target. For example: "We'll install a solar PV system when it can pay for itself in less than eight years." ☐

Chris: Yes, that seems reasonable to me.

Amy: That seems a good compromise to me. So, let's move on to the next item on the agenda …

B Smart energy solutions

1

12

Listening: a teleconference

Listen carefully, then complete the sentences with information from the conversation.

1 The purpose of the teleconference is to discuss …

_____

_____

2 The board likes the solar installation because …

_____

3 The board wants to look at …

_____

4 The power bill for the Bonn datacentre last year …

_____

5 The four biggest energy uses were …

_____

> *Mit Hör- / Sehverstehensaufgaben umgehen: SB p. 215*

2

If-sentences type II: what would happen if …?

Use the key words to write if-sentences type II.

1 we • install • LED lighting • save • a lot of energy

_____

2 Jim • get • a PV system • not live • in an apartment building

_____

3 Micro-CHPs • be • cheaper • I • buy • one

_____

4 the server room • get • very hot • cooling system • fail

_____

5 our company • want • to save energy • install • occupancy monitors

_____

6 the solar panels • on our roof • not generate • power • be • in the shade

_____

7 our PV system • be • independent of the grid • we • have • large batteries

_____

8 you • have • a stand-alone PV system • you • have to • replace • the batteries • after several years

_____

> *If-sentences: SB p. 230*

3 **Reading: saving energy**

A Read the following article from a magazine for business managers, then choose the most suitable endings to finish the sentences about the text.

Small changes to make big savings

Saving energy in the office is not just for big business: it is even more important for small companies, argues energy efficiency expert Marta Jones. "Some simple changes can lower your energy costs dramatically," says Jones. "Many of them are a matter of changing employee behaviour rather than installing new technology."

Without computers, routers, photocopiers and printers, companies just couldn't conduct their business. Yet all of these machines use energy, and together may account for more than 18 per cent of a company's power bill, the latest figures from the Environment Protection Agency show. They also contribute significantly to emissions of greenhouse gases.

With this in mind, there is no point in wasting energy on machines which are not in use. "Tell your employees to turn off their computers if they are going to be away from their desk for more than 30 minutes," advises Jones. "That can save several hours of power usage every week." Most modern computers have a "power down" feature to shut down automatically, but it is even better to switch off the machine at the power point, because electrical equipment still uses power in standby mode.

Jones thinks that bosses should encourage employees to have realistic expectations about heating and cooling: "Does the office really need to stay at a warm 21 degrees in the middle of winter? Wouldn't 18 degrees be better for concentration? Watch out for employees opening windows – maybe it's time to turn down the heating!"

Lighting is another big energy use for business. Fortunately companies can achieve big savings – about 50 per cent – by installing LEDs instead of fluorescent tube lighting. "You will save even more if you encourage employees to turn off unneeded lights," reminds Jones. Timers and occupancy monitors are other options to make sure that the lights go off when the workers go home.

(312 words)

1   According to Marta Jones …

   a   installing new technology is the main way to reduce power costs.   ☐
   b   employees do not care about wasting power.   ☐
   c   businesses do not need to install new technology to reduce power costs.   ☐

2   Information technology …

   a   is almost 20 per cent of a company's power use.   ☐
   b   uses nearly 20 per cent more power than in the past.   ☐
   c   can reduce a company's power costs by nearly 20 per cent.   ☐

3   The article suggests that employees should …

   a   set their computers to power down automatically when they aren't using them.   ☐
   b   turn off their computers at the power point rather than setting them to power down.   ☐
   c   not leave their desks for more than 30 minutes during working hours.   ☐

4   Jones thinks that office workers …

   a   will work harder if they are not too warm.   ☐
   b   should open the windows if they are too hot.   ☐
   c   should take more responsibility for controlling the office temperature.   ☐

5   Suggested ways to save on lighting include …

   a   telling workers to go home on time.   ☐
   b   installing fluorescent tubes.   ☐
   c   using automatic sensors.   ☐

B What do you think of the advice? Consider the viewpoints of employers and employees. Write a short comment on the text.

C The way forward

1 **Word power: renewable energy**

Complete the sentences. The first letter of each word has been given to help you. All the words can be found on page 134 of the Student's Book.

1 When an electric vehicle runs out of energy, you have to c_____ its batteries.

2 It is necessary to b_____ the electrical grid, so that supply and demand are equal.

3 Our homes are full of a_____ such as refrigerators, washing machines and TVs which run on electricity.

4 Ethanol is an example of a b_____ – it can be made from maize, sugar or other plant material.

5 Both the sun and the wind are i_____ energy sources, yet we need electricity all the time.

6 Thanks to its many rivers and lakes, Austria is one of the biggest producers of h_____ power in Europe.

7 The lights all over the city went out in the p_____ c_____ last night.

8 Batteries are a useful form of energy s_____: by turning electrical energy into chemical energy, we can keep it until it is needed.

---

2 **Mediation**

Ein deutscher Freund bestreitet, dass Solarenergie einen bedeutenden Beitrag zum Energiemix machen kann. Widerlegen Sie seine Ansicht in einer E-Mail anhand der Informationen im folgenden Zeitungsartikel. Übersetzen Sie dabei nicht Wort für Wort.

UK and Germany break solar power records
John Vidal

Britain and Germany have broken records for generating solar electricity in the last few weeks, according to new industry figures. Basking in[1] the sunniest weather of summer during the longest days of the year, Germany generated over half its electricity demand from solar on a single day on 9 June and the UK nearly doubled its 2013 peak[2] solar power output at the solstice[3] weekend (21–22 June).

France, Italy, Denmark and other countries are also believed to have generated record amounts in June.

According to UK trade body[4] the Solar Trade association (STA), the total UK installed solar capacity generated from homes, buildings and solar farms is now about 4.7 gigawatts (GW) compared to 2.7 GW in July last year.

It is not possible to tell exactly how much solar power was generated in Britain because electricity from small-scale household units is not centrally measured, but the STA estimated on Monday that 3.9% of the UK's electricity demand was met by solar photovoltaic systems (PV) over the 24 hours of Saturday.

This means solar's contribution peaked at a record 7.8% of daytime electricity on 21 June, said the association.

"Britain has virtually doubled its capacity in the last year, with 80,000 more installations, including several thousand larger scale commercial ones," said Ray Noble, a consultant at the UK National Solar Centre.

"There are now 530,000 installations in the UK, of which 510,000 are domestic small scale ones. Last weekend we estimate they generated about 8% of daytime electricity in total," said Noble. "We think that this is likely to double again within a year. There is nothing to stop it getting to 30-40% of UK electricity at this time of year," he said.

Germany, with 1.4 million PV systems, generated a peak of 23.1 GW hours at lunchtime on Monday 9 June, equivalent to 50.6% of its total electricity need. According to government development agency Germany Trade and Invest (GTAI), solar power grew 34% in the first five months of 2014 compared to last year.   (338 words)

[1] genießen, wörtlich: sich sonnen; [2] Spitzen-
[3] Sonnenwende; [4] Industrieverband

abridged and adapted from
www.theguardian.com, 23.06.2014

3

Describing a cartoon

Describe and analyse the cartoon. Compare it with the text. Use the framework below to structure your essay.

Step 1: Describe the cartoon.

The cartoon shows _____

_____

_____

The pilot is making an announcement, explaining _____

_____

_____

_____

> SO WE'RE PREDICTING A NICE COMFORTABLE FLIGHT TODAY FOLKS, UNLESS OF COURSE WE RUN INTO ANY CLOUD COVER

Step 2: Interpret the cartoon.

The message of the cartoon is that _____

_____

_____

_____

Step 3: Compare and contrast the cartoon with the text.

Although the cartoon suggests that _____ ,

_____

the text tells us that _____

_____

Step 4: Give your opinion.

The cartoonist is right / partly right / completely wrong about solar power for aircraft: _____

_____

_____

> Bilder und Cartoons beschreiben und analysieren: SB p. 218

Solar Impulse

In 2013 the solar electric aircraft Solar Impulse flew across the United States from San Francisco to New York in several stages. Solar Impulse is able to fly day and night, charging its batteries in flight. The new Solar Impulse 2 has the same wingspan as an Airbus 380, the world's largest passenger aircraft, but only weighs the same as a car and can carry only one person, the pilot.

12 Tomorrow's world

A Cloud computing

1 Word power: cloud computing

A Match the following collocations to their definitions. Use the internet for help, if necessary.

1	open source	a	when all the computers on a network work together to solve a problem
2	service migration	b	large volumes of structured or unstructured data
3	MySQL	c	a company that provides cloud services
4	cloud provider	d	to move your cloud from one vendor to another
5	big data	e	a cloud that can only be accessed by certain individuals
6	grid computing	f	a piece of software whose source code is available for anyone to use
7	private cloud	g	an open source database system

1	2	3	4	5	6	7

B Complete the sentences using the collocations from 1A.

1 We have a lot of _____ . We need to outsource it for processing.

2 Our databases are maintained on _____ , because it is cheaper than a private database system.

3 An _____ application is cheaper than a private application, but the support systems are not as good.

4 We are not happy with our cloud provider, so we are thinking about _____ .

5 Our _____ charges us a monthly fee and gives us full round-the-clock technical support.

6 We used to be on an open cloud, but due to increased security requirements, we have switched to a

_____ .

2 Listening: future trends

13

A Listen to the podcast and choose the most suitable option.

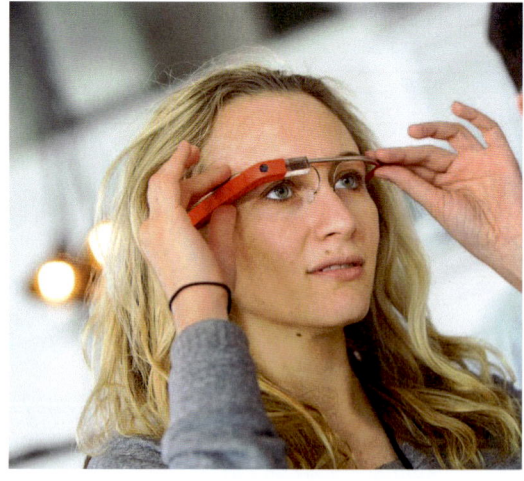

1 The presenter's name is
   a Simon Schott   c Simon Hot
   b Simon Scott   d Simon Stott

2 The basic computer used to be
   a a PC   c a laptop
   b a games console   d a calculator

3 Your car will drive automatically to
   a the gas station you have programmed it to drive to
   b the nearest gas station with the best quality gas
   c your favourite gas station
   d the nearest gas station with the cheapest gas

4 Tesco is
   a an English retailer   c a British retailer
   b an Irish retailer   d a French retailer

5 The aim of all this ground breaking technology is
   a to boost health   c to boost wealth
   b to boost sales   d to boost education

B Listen again and answer the questions.

1   What is Ellen Diaz an expert on?

   _____

2   Why is having a lot more computers in the future a problem?

   _____

3   What examples does Ellen Diaz give of household appliances with computers that interact with each other?

   _____

4   What will companies have to do to differently because of this interconnectedness?

   _____

5   What will companies be able to do with all this extra data?

   _____

6   What will the software do if it thinks the person is sad, excited, or tired?

   _____

3   **Talking about the future**

A   Choose the correct form to complete these descriptions of plans and predictions. Sometimes both forms are possible, but one form is better than the other.

1   According to this programme, Simon (will talk / is going to talk) to Ellen Diaz about e-business and digital communications technology today.
2   Ellen thinks that cloud computing (will be / is going to be) the answer to storing large amounts of data.
3   Based on current data, she knows that there (will be / are going to be) a lot more computers in the future.
4   She imagines that in the future all sorts of household appliances (will have / are going to have) computers that (will / are going to) interact with each other.
5   Tesco has announced that it (will introduce / is going to introduce) eye scanners at gas stations.
6   If companies have data on our shopping habits, they (will / are going to) use them to target us with customized advertising.

B   Sort the sentences above into the correct category.

a   a description of a plan: _____

b   a prediction that is based on firm evidence: _____

c   a prediction that is not based on firm evidence: _____

C   What about you? Answer the following questions using 'will' and 'going to'.

1   What are you going to do this weekend?
2   Are you going to do your homework for tomorrow?
3   Are you going to go to a party on Saturday?
4   Where do you think you will be living in five years?
5   What do you think you will be doing in ten years?
6   Do you think you will be married in fifteen years?

B Where are we heading?

1

Word power: jobs for the future

A Complete the sentences using job titles from the box.

> body part maker • caring animal trainer • holistic carer • occupational therapist •
> physiotherapist • wellness consultant

1 A/An _____ creates organs or limbs for people who have chronic ailments or have

   been injured.

2 A/An _____ encourages and assists people to take part in everyday activities even

   though their physical or mental abilities may be impaired.

3 A/An _____ helps people to live a healthy lifestyle by advising on diet, exercise,

   stress management, coping skills and on how to avoid addictions.

4 A/An _____ teaches special carers how to support clients in their homes and

   everyday life.

5 A/An _____ treats injury or dysfunction with exercises and other physical treatment.

6 A/An _____ treats symptoms but also looks for underlying causes of these symptoms.

2

14

Listening: the future of learning

Listen to Wayne Gale talking to Madeline Jameson about
virtual high schools and match the two halves of
these statements.

1 Full-time virtual education has become very popular
   and successful in the States,
2 In our virtual schools, children who progress at their
   own speed
3 Virtual education has become an alternative
4 We are using modern technology to deliver quality
   education to any child,
5 Co-operative problem solving, and working with other people is key not just to the global economy
6 In the primary classes, the model relies on the intensive work of a parent
7 These weak results are related to the fact that our program
8 If you take students who would normally struggle because of their home environment and then you leave
   them at home to learn,

a to traditional schools for an increasingly wide selection of students.
b do their learning largely independently, with lessons delivered online.
c who has to act as a "learning coach."
d but to getting along in life.
e you shouldn't be surprised if it doesn't work that well.
f often attracts students who struggle in regular schools.
g upending the traditional American notion that learning occurs in a school building where students share
   the experience.
h regardless of where he or she lives.

1	2	3	4	5	6	7	8

3 **Reading: three interesting professions**

› *Schwierige Texte lesen: SB p. 210*

A Rick, Jill and Thomas were asked to describe their jobs for an online magazine. Unfortunately their texts have got jumbled. Put the text segments in order (from 1–9), then write a job title from exercise 1 next to each of the names.

Rick _____   Jill _____   Thomas _____

1 People in this profession can also work in the world of fitness. I trained as a nutritionist and have a certificate from the National Association for Fitness which allows me to work in the areas of Fitness Assessment, Lifestyle Consulting and

4 We are still at the research and development stage. There are huge advances being made in bio-tissues, robotics and plastics, and the creation of organs and limbs will soon be possible. A typical organ such as a liver or kidney might be grown in a laboratory

7 We do this because we believe that there is a link between our physical health and our general well-being. Our physical, psychological, emotional, social, spiritual and environmental states are all interconnected so they have to be managed together

☐ a to keep the client well. When a patient comes in with a physical symptom, for example, stomach problems, and the doctor knows that the patient has a stressful job, then the problems might be relieved by teaching the patient anti-stress techniques. I have a general

☐ b in private practice is finding clients who can afford the service if they don't have insurance or if their insurance does not cover a consultation. People don't want to pay privately.

☐ c under strictly controlled conditions. We have already developed intelligent arm and hand prosthetics using robotic joints but we are still working on developing other parts such as artificially grown skin and synthetic flesh and muscles. We are not quite there yet and we are always worried about

☐ d medical degree and I worked in the local hospital for two years. Now I'm building up a practice with two colleagues. We're sure it's going to be a success. After a long time relying on orthodox medicine*, people are returning to natural ways of healing. The problem is, of course, not everyone has the money to pay for the treatment.   * *Schulmedizin*

☐ e where to get funding. I trained as a medical laboratory assistant and got this job not long after I qualified. I hope that one day, I'll be able to help people like my brother, who lost an arm in an accident.

☐ f Nutrition Analysis. At the moment, I work in a fitness centre but my dream is to become a private consultant, providing fitness assessments and training to individuals. The challenge

B Answer the following questions based on the texts. The information in the texts is not always in the same order as the questions.

1 *What training did the individuals have which makes them suitable for their work? What are their qualifications?*

2 *Where do they work?*

3 *What do they think about their future?*

C Drones take off

1 **Watching a video: "Drones for hire"**

Watch the video, then answer the questions below.

2:32

1 Why has the use of civilian drones increased?

_____

2 Who were Daniel Garate's main customers?

_____

3 What did the Los Angelese Police Department (LAPD)

recently stop? _____

4 What is Cy Brown's "Dehogaflier"? _____

5 Where and how was the "Robocopter" used? _____

6 Where could people view Team Blacksheep's film? _____

7 What don't the authorities like? _____

2 **Word power: drones**

Complete the dialogue with the English translations of the words in brackets.

Ⓐ Using drones to _____[1] (*aufnehmen*) sporting events is an interesting idea, but I'm not sure that

I like the idea of drones where there are _____[2] (*Menschenmengen*).

Ⓑ How do you mean?

Ⓐ If the operator doesn't know what he or she is doing, and _____[3] (*die Kontrolle verlieren über*) the drone, it could easily injure someone.

Ⓑ True. But some drones have _____[4] (*Gefahrvermeidung*) technology now. So they're able

to fly _____[5] (*autonom*), even in a _____[6] (*bebautes Gebiet*).

Ⓐ Well, what if a drone _____[7] (*einer Drohne der Treibstoff ausgeht*)? It could

_____[8] (*abstürzen*) and injure someone.

Ⓑ Also true. But civilian drones are generally too small and light to be really dangerous. And maybe we'll see more

_____[9] (*solarbetrieben*) drones in the future, too. Personally I think drones have a great

future – for replacing conventional _____[10] (*Kurierdienste*), for example.

Ⓐ Don't you think that's just a _____[11] (*Werbetrick*) by a few companies that want

publicity? The range of drones is very low, it would only be practical to run a drone delivery service in an

_____[12] (*Stadtgebiet*), close to the store.

Ⓑ Think about the traffic in our cities, though. It's time-consuming and expensive to deliver packages by road.

The _____[13] (*Versandkosten*) would be much lower for delivery by drone.

Ⓐ Maybe, but what about _____[14] (*Privatsphäre*)? People wouldn't like drones buzzing by their

windows all the time – they would wonder whether the drones _____[15] (*ausspionierten*)

them …

3 **Mind map: civilian drones**   > *Mindmaps und Gliederungen erstellen: SB p. 215*

A Complete this mind map with your own ideas about civilian drones.

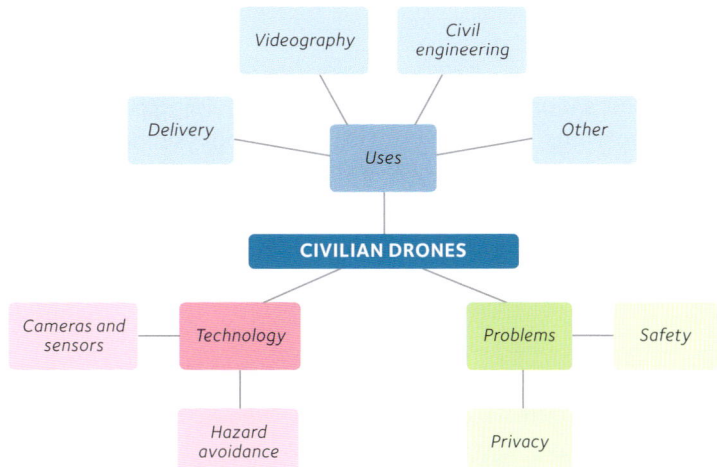

B Using the mind map you created in 3A, discuss the advantages and disadvantages of civilian drones.
Write 200–250 words.   > *Einen Aufsatz oder eine Stellungnahme schreiben: SB p. 216*

4 **Predicting the future**

A In your opinion, will these things happen in the next ten years? Give each scenario a score out of 5.
(1 = definitely no, 5 = definitely yes)

Scenario	Score				
	1	2	3	4	5
1 Drones replace human police officers.	☐	☐	☐	☐	☐
2 Drones do our daily shopping for us.	☐	☐	☐	☐	☐
3 Civilian drones are banned in Europe.	☐	☐	☐	☐	☐
4 Drones are used for parcel delivery.	☐	☐	☐	☐	☐
5 Video drones are used at all sporting events.	☐	☐	☐	☐	☐
6 Drones are an important tool for search and rescue missions.	☐	☐	☐	☐	☐
7 Drones protect national parks from fires and vandals.	☐	☐	☐	☐	☐
8 There are more drones than cars in our cities.	☐	☐	☐	☐	☐
9 Every household has at least one drone.	☐	☐	☐	☐	☐
10 Drone pilots need an operator's licence.	☐	☐	☐	☐	☐

B Write predictions using your scores from the quiz and the following verb forms.

Score	Verb form
1	isn't/aren't going to
2	probably won't
3	might/may
4	probably will
5	is/are going to

Example: Drones replace human police officers. (Score = 2)
Drones probably won't replace human police officers.

1 Mit unbekannten Wörtern umgehen

> Mit unbekannten Wörtern umgehen: SB p. 210
> weitere Beispielaufgaben: SB p. 18

SITUATION You are attending a careers workshop which is aimed at helping prospective care professionals decide on their field of caring. In this part of the workshop, you have been asked to find a text about a caring professional at work and give a short talk on what they do. You have chosen the text below.

A Read the text and decide if the following statements are true or false. Give reasons for all of your answers.

		True	False
1	At the start of her shift, Marilyn gets information about the patients from the night staff.		
2	Elias has been told that the terminal illness he has is getting worse faster than expected.		
3	Cora is relieved that her mother has died and is no longer in pain.		
4	Before she comforts somebody, Marilyn thinks about what she is feeling so she can tell the person about her own fears.		
5	Marilyn teaches trainees to be aware of their own culture.		

Scenes from the life of a palliative care worker
Marilyn Page

People often take a deep breath when I tell them what I do. Then they ask me how I cope with death day in, day out. They don't understand that working in palliative care is more than dealing with a death. It
5 is about supporting people to live their lives notwithstanding the diagnosis they've been given. Palliative care supports people in their wish to die what they themselves define as a "good death"; it also helps families cope with the loss of their loved
10 ones.

I work in a local hospice. During the handover this morning, I heard that Elias had bad news about the progression of his disease. He had been optimistic about a study he was participating in but is now
15 struggling to accept the blow. The question which many patients with chronic diseases often have is "Why me?" There is no answer to that one. I just have to sit with Elias while he goes over his fears.

Later, I spend an hour sitting in the hospice garden with Cora, the daughter of a patient who has just
20 died. The teenager is devastated by the loss of her mother. My role is simply to be here for her. Palliative care workers are trained in active listening and that is what we do. The session is about Cora, not about me. Before I have a session like this, I mull
25 over my own feelings about the situation then I put these feelings to one side. It is the feelings of the bereaved that matter, not mine. Sessions like these are emotionally draining but very gratifying.

Before I go home, I give a talk to trainees about
30 cultural competence in palliative care. I remind them that they first need to be cognizant of their own cultural values in order to be able to understand people from other cultures. I enjoy teaching the trainees. They are the next generation of palliative
35 care workers. I like passing on my knowledge and experience to them. (333 words)

B Find synonyms in the text for the following words and expressions.

1 every day for a long period of time _____

_____

2 despite _____

3 to take part in _____

4 to reflect on _____

5 exhausting _____

6 rewarding _____

2 Präsentieren
3 Mindmaps und Gliederungen erstellen

> Präsentieren: SB p. 217

> Mindmaps und Gliederungen erstellen: SB p. 215

> weitere Beispielaufgaben: SB p. 30/42

SITUATION You work for a German organization which finds people who would like to act as mentors to migrants who might need support. In order to give prospective volunteers an insight into the background of the clients and their problems, your boss has asked you to prepare a presentation.

A Using information from a variety of sources, including the texts on these two pages, make a mind map about migration, e.g. who the migrants are, where they come from, what their problems are in their homelands and what awaits them in Germany.

A boy tells his story

"There was always trouble in my country. After my parents disappeared, I went with my grandparents to a camp. The camp was bombed and we had to move on. I don't know how it happened, but I lost my grandparents so, instead of going to a new camp, I just kept walking. When I was in the first camp, I heard that Denmark was a safe place to go so I thought I would go there. I don't know how long I was walking. I slept in barns and stole food to eat. I was caught by the border police when I tried to come into Germany. Now I'm living in a children's home in Regensburg. It's OK here. I have a bed and get lessons at school. I miss my family but I don't miss my country. I have applied for asylum but my social worker says it will take a long time before my case comes up."

Asylum seekers – Where are they from? What have they suffered?

Many of the people seeking asylum in Germany come from conflict areas like the Central African Republic. The conflict there started at the end of 2012. During June – August 2013 there were reports of over 200,000 internally displaced persons (IDPs) as well as human rights abuses including the use of child soldiers, rape, torture, extrajudicial killings and forced disappearances. In 2014, Amnesty International reported several massacres committed by the Christian group called Anti-balaka against Muslim civilians, forcing thousands of Muslims to flee the country.

+13% – Immigration to Germany at its highest rate
Immigration to Germany increased by 13% in 2013, reaching 1,226,000 people, the **highest peak since 1993**. The same year 789,000 persons left the country (+11%), with a balance of +437,000. These figures were released by the Federal Statistical Office, which highlights that a large majority of the immigrants (1,108 million people, 15% more compared to 2012) have foreign citizenship, mostly from the **EU countries**. Especially **Italy** and **Spain** fueled the boom, with increases by 52% and 19% of emigrants. The data show a sharp growth in **refugees** from nations in war: e.g. Syria (17 thousand people, + 133%), Somalia (4,000, +395%), Egypt (4,000, +180%) and Libya (3,000, +173%).

http://www.west-info.eu/west-news/topics/immigration-topics/

Lebensbedingungen von Asylbewerbern

Asylbewerber erhalten eine vorläufige Aufenthaltserlaubnis und einen Wohnort zugewiesen, den sie nicht verlassen dürfen. Sie werden in Sammelunterkünften untergebracht und mit Sachgütern sowie Taschengeld versorgt. Zu arbeiten ist ihnen verboten. Dies ändert sich erst, wenn sie als asylberechtigt anerkannt werden oder Flüchtlingsschutz erhalten. Das Bundesverfassungsgericht hat 2012 festgelegt, dass die staatlichen Hilfen für Asylbewerber und Flüchtlinge auf das Niveau der Grundsicherung für Deutsche angehoben werden müssen.

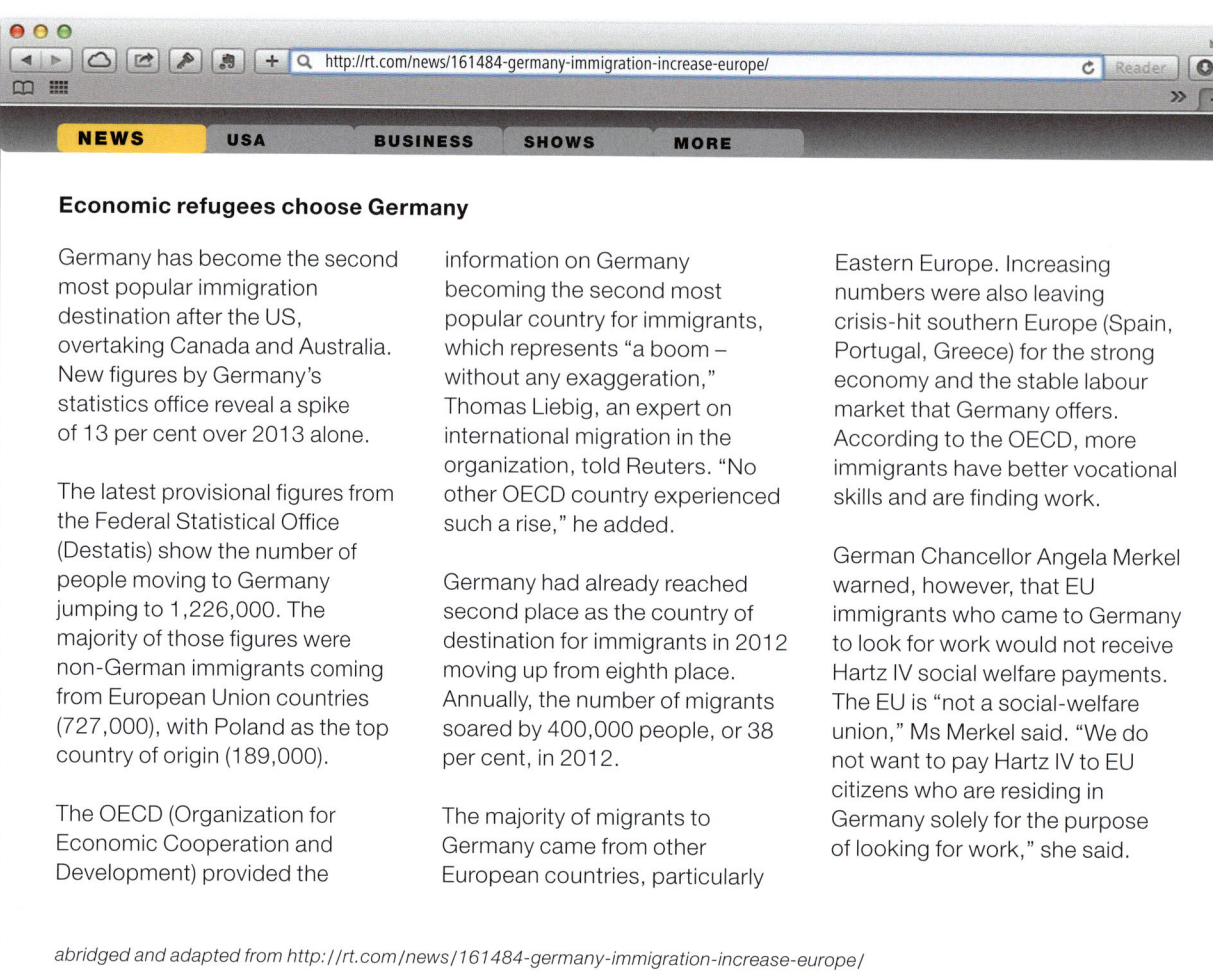

http://rt.com/news/161484-germany-immigration-increase-europe/

NEWS   USA   BUSINESS   SHOWS   MORE

Economic refugees choose Germany

Germany has become the second most popular immigration destination after the US, overtaking Canada and Australia. New figures by Germany's statistics office reveal a spike of 13 per cent over 2013 alone.

The latest provisional figures from the Federal Statistical Office (Destatis) show the number of people moving to Germany jumping to 1,226,000. The majority of those figures were non-German immigrants coming from European Union countries (727,000), with Poland as the top country of origin (189,000).

The OECD (Organization for Economic Cooperation and Development) provided the information on Germany becoming the second most popular country for immigrants, which represents "a boom – without any exaggeration," Thomas Liebig, an expert on international migration in the organization, told Reuters. "No other OECD country experienced such a rise," he added.

Germany had already reached second place as the country of destination for immigrants in 2012 moving up from eighth place. Annually, the number of migrants soared by 400,000 people, or 38 per cent, in 2012.

The majority of migrants to Germany came from other European countries, particularly Eastern Europe. Increasing numbers were also leaving crisis-hit southern Europe (Spain, Portugal, Greece) for the strong economy and the stable labour market that Germany offers. According to the OECD, more immigrants have better vocational skills and are finding work.

German Chancellor Angela Merkel warned, however, that EU immigrants who came to Germany to look for work would not receive Hartz IV social welfare payments. The EU is "not a social-welfare union," Ms Merkel said. "We do not want to pay Hartz IV to EU citizens who are residing in Germany solely for the purpose of looking for work," she said.

abridged and adapted from http://rt.com/news/161484-germany-immigration-increase-europe/

B Using your mind map and the template below, outline the situation for migrants in Germany as you would like to describe it in your presentation.

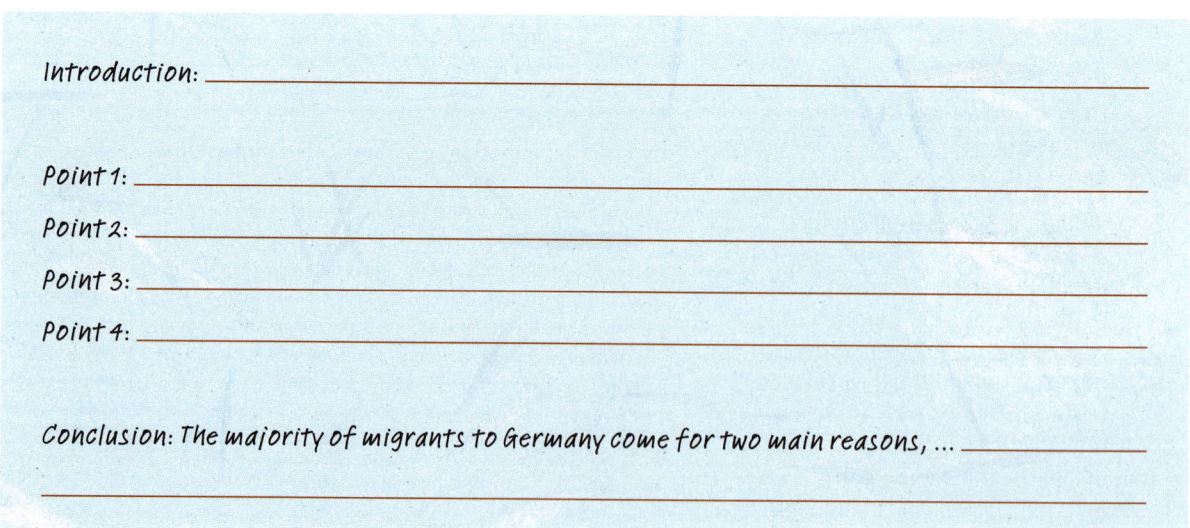

Introduction: _____

Point 1: _____

Point 2: _____

Point 3: _____

Point 4: _____

Conclusion: The majority of migrants to Germany come for two main reasons, ... _____
_____

C Think of an interesting title for your presentation and create four presentation slides. Make your slides lively, interesting and eye-catching. Use as few words as possible.

4 Textproduktion – Umgang mit Operatoren

> Textproduktion – Umgang mit Operatoren: SB p. 210
> weitere Beispielaufgaben: SB p. 54

SITUATION You work in an organization which cares for at-risk teens. There has been a lot of discussion in the media lately about the pros and cons of legalizing drugs. Your boss has called a meeting to discuss the issues. In preparation for the meeting, you read a comment in *The Guardian* from a journalist who is against decriminalizing cannabis, also called marijuana or pot.

Read the following extract from the comment, in which the writer attacks a Conservative Member of the European Parliament (MEP) who is for the legislation of drugs. Then do the following tasks.

1 Outline the author's main arguments.
2 Find evidence in the text to show how decriminalization affects drug use.
3 Describe the health risks of smoking cannabis according to the text.
4 Say what has been happening in Colorado schools since legalization.
5 Assess the author's arguments and decide if you agree or disagree with them.

Legalizing drugs would bring not freedom but enslavement

Kathy Gyngell for ConservativeHome

I can only assume that Daniel Hannan [the conservative MEP who is for legislation] is unaware of the consequences of Brixton's cannabis decriminalization experiment and of the later temporary nationwide declassification of cannabis. I guess he does not know that immediate rises in consumption of 25% and 30% took place, nor how long it took for analysis of this to reach the public domain.

I doubt he knows of the 2013 testing of the wider impact of the Brixton experiment. The key finding was a dramatic rise in hospital admissions of 15- to 34-year-old class A drug users. They were 40–100% more likely to be admitted during the policy trial – a period in which police were told to ignore street level cannabis offences.

Like many people, Hannan is probably also unaware that [over the last 15 years] in the United States, when 21 states legalized so-called medical marijuana, teenage drug use doubled to much higher levels than here and was accompanied by a halving of teens' perception of harm. People know little of the greatly enhanced cancer risks of smoking cannabis, its effects on the adolescent brain – on motivation, IQ, psychosis and schizophrenia – or that naming cannabis as an official cause of death is increasing.

According to Dr Christian Thurstone, the director of one of Colorado's largest youth substance-abuse treatment clinics, regular high school drug use has leaped from 19% to 30% since Colorado legalized medical marijuana in 2009 for adults; teens are using more higher potency products; school expulsions are up by a third, and 74% of teens in his drug-treatment clinic are using somebody else's medical marijuana, all of it diverted through somebody who is 18 or older.

> The Brixton cannabis decriminalization programme was launched on 2 July 2001 and lasted six months. Under the scheme, no one was arrested or charged for possessing the drug.

Since full legalization, the school situation in Colorado has got worse. "Kids are smoking before school and during lunch breaks. They come into school stinking of pot," school resource officers say. "Students don't seem to realize that there is anything wrong with having it … they act like having marijuana was an ordinary thing and no big deal".

To return to the current situation in Britain, young people here are more, not less, responsible than before: they drink less, use drugs less, commit fewer crimes and volunteer more, as a recent Demos report shows. In these newly competitive times, the last thing this generation need is having a drugs-legalizing experiment forced on them by ageing politicians.

Hannan might not mind exposing his children to this experiment. I think most parents would.

(456 words)

abridged and adapted from The Guardian, Guardian Comment Network, 20.02.2014

5 Einen Aufsatz oder eine Stellungnahme schreiben

> Einen Aufsatz oder eine Stellungnahme schreiben: SB p. 216
> weitere Beispielaufgaben: SB p. 66

SITUATION You work for an organization which assists older people who are having difficulties finding employment. You find the following article online and decide to post it with a comment on your organization's intranet.

A Read the text and choose the best summary from the options below.

1 Online applications might help older job seekers in their hopes for work.
2 Older job seekers have better chances during a recession.
3 Age-discrimination laws don't help when HR managers are prejudiced.

Survey throws an interesting light on ageism

A recent UK survey, which was carried out by a demographic institute, looked into how 45-to-74-year-old unemployed job seekers got on when looking for employment. Among the people who ⁵ took part in the survey, nearly one in five of the job seekers believed that they had been turned down for employment because of their age. The researchers also asked employers about their attitudes to employing people in the 45-to-74 age ¹⁰ group.

According to this part of the survey, many HR managers appear to have wrong ideas about older employees which affect the chances of older applicants when they apply for a position. ¹⁵ Two of the problems most often stated by HR managers were that older candidates are less likely to be willing to give their time and energy to the company and that they are not as productive as younger employees.

²⁰ More worrying than these misconceptions, the researchers discovered that age discrimination laws were ignored.

In the conclusion of the survey, the researcher in charge of the project said: "We have found ²⁵ evidence that age discrimination laws do not appear to benefit older workers, and jobless rates for older workers look to remain high. The situation is worse for female workers than it is for men."

³⁰ A spokesperson for the institute which carried out the survey said: "Employers dismiss the accusation that they are ignoring age-discrimination legislation. Many of them point out that using online applications, they have no way to find out how old an applicant ³⁵ is. On the other hand, even though applicants do not always have to include their date of birth on an application, graduation dates or dates of employment will always give a hint at an applicant's age. In some cases, of course, ⁴⁰ employers ask job seekers to enter their date of birth on online applications," the spokesperson continued. "If they do not enter the information, they can't move on to the next screen and finish the application process. A reply to an ⁴⁵ unsuccessful online application will never explain why the application has been rejected," she concluded.

A spokesperson for Age Ability, an organization which helps older job seekers find work, explained: "Things are particularly ⁵⁰ difficult during an economic recession. As the economy becomes weaker, the numbers of complaints about age discrimination rise. Older job applicants are the first to be rejected because ⁵⁵ of the mistaken belief that they will not be productive. What managers forget to take into account is the fact that older workers, with all their years of experience, might help a company to weather the storms of a recession and come ⁶⁰ out of it in a better state than a company which employs only younger people." (448 words)

B Comment on this statement: "Both older applicants and HR managers would improve the state of business if employers threw out their mistaken ideas about the abilities of older workers."

6 Schwierige Texte lesen

> Schwierige Texte lesen: SB p. 210
> weitere Beispielaufgaben: SB p. 78

SITUATION The Department of City Planning has recently received many complaints about the number of outdoor adverts appearing in the city. The head of the department has asked you to research how other cities deal with the issue and report back to her. During the research, you discover an interesting article on São Paulo's advertising ban.

A Read the article and select the correct answer to the statements below.

1 Until one hundred years ago, no city in the world had …
   a billboard adverts   b electricity   c running water   d lost and found adverts

2 The city of São Paulo passed a _____ ban on advertising in 2006.
   a duvet   b carpet   c blanket   d cover

3 In 2006, the mayor of São Paulo passed the …
   a New City Law   b Clean City Law   c Blanket City Law   d Dirty City Law

4 In 2011, a poll showed that _____ % of São Paulo's residents were in favour of the ban.
   a 11   b 3   c 70   d 60

The city that said "no" to advertising

The concept of advertising is thousands of years old: ancient Egyptians advertised their products on papyrus and on the walls of their shops, archaeologists have found political adverts in Pompeii and ancient Arabia and lost and found ads were normal in ancient Rome and Greece.

The advertising industry, however, is something new. In today's world, ads have become one of the most visible aspects of modern life. Can you imagine a city where there are no billboards urging you to buy things or telling you where to get the best deals in town? Until one hundred years ago, no city in the world had such adverts, but today you have to travel far to find a city free of advertising.

While there are several cities that have rejected outdoor advertising, the biggest by far is São Paulo. Brazil's second-largest city and the financial capital of the country instigated* a blanket ban on outdoor advertising in 2006. The people of the city felt overwhelmed by the number of billboards they saw everywhere they looked, so mayor Gilberto Kassab passed the "Clean City Law" and overnight all the outdoor adverts were removed.

Opponents of the ban feared São Paulo would lose much of its income and become a drab and boring place without the colourful adverts to catch one's eye. However, a poll in 2011 showed that 70% of the city's 11 million residents were in favour of the ban. The city could once again display its rich architectural heritage, they said. And the city has survived just fine without the revenue gained from outdoor advertising. A side-effect of the ban is that the poverty-stricken slums that were once hidden by giant signs have now been exposed. Because they can no longer be overlooked, they have sparked a debate among the people of the city about how to address the issue of extreme poverty and politicians have begun searching for permanent, long-term solutions.

São Paulo's experiment has inspired an anti-advertising movement. In Bergen, Norway, outdoor adverts are banned around the city and a quick tour with Google Streetview confirms that the city still is beautiful despite the lack of consumerist messages. In the USA, the states of Hawaii, Vermont and Alaska have banned outdoor advertising and cities like Auckland (New Zealand) and Chennai (India) also have restrictions in place. The argument is that while you can choose which adverts to watch on TV and which adverts to read in magazines, you cannot choose which adverts to see on the street.

(419 words)

* initiieren / anregen

B Discuss the advantages and disadvantages of an advertising ban.

7 Mit Hör-/Sehverstehensaufgaben umgehen

> *Mit Hör-/Sehverstehensaufgaben umgehen: SB p. 215*
> *weitere Beispielaufgaben: SB p. 90*

SITUATION You have almost finished your studies and are thinking about volunteering, not only to do good, but also to gain experience. You do research on the internet and find a podcast and a video with interesting and useful information.

15

A You first find a podcast in which Mark from the Pulse team interviews Anne, a volunteer at a hostel for asylum seekers.

First, read the questions, then listen carefully to the interview and make notes. Then listen again and answer the questions in English. The answers to some of the questions may be in different parts of the interview.

1 Warum wollte Anne ehrenamtlich arbeiten?
2 Warum nahm sie sich ausreichend Zeit, um zu entscheiden, wo sie arbeiten möchte?
3 Mit wem arbeitet Anne in dem Heim?
4 Was möchten Freiwillige die mit genau diesen Klienten arbeiten, erreichen?
5 Wie machen Freiwillige das?
6 Was machte Anne in Afrika?
7 Um wen kümmerte sie sich dort?
8 Wie nutzte die Organisation die Kinder aus?
9 Wie machte sich die Organisation Anne und die anderen Freiwilligen zunutze?
10 Wie können Interessierte, die ehrenamtlich arbeiten möchten, sicherstellen, dass sie nicht von FreiwilligenOrganisationen ausgenutzt werden?

B Choose the most suitable title for the podcast from the list below.

1 A way to fill up your CV
2 Help disadvantaged children and help yourself find your place
3 Proving that you're willing to work
4 The importance of choosing the right volunteer organization
5 Volunteering: a way to find out if the job is right for you
6 Volunteering doesn't only mean teaching kids

6

C Next, you watch the video "Youth in Action – EVS for volunteers". Read the tasks below and make notes to help you to answer them. You can watch the video twice.

1 Say what the video is about.
2 Explain why it is difficult for the asylum seekers to become integrated with the local people.
3 Describe the families who live in the centre and point out the problem the younger children face. Find evidence in the video to show how the volunteers deal with the children's problems.
4 Point out how the volunteers interact with the adults in the centre.
5 Describe some of the benefits to young volunteers of programmes like this.
6 Comment on how volunteer involvement in similar refugee centres might help refugees in the future.

8 An Diskussionen teilnehmen

> An Diskussionen teilnehmen: SB p. 218
> weitere Beispielaufgaben: SB p. 102

SITUATION Briefcase Travel, a medium-sized travel company based in Kent, organizes exclusive business travel for companies and individual business people. In the last quarter, the company has seen a significant drop in sales due to increased competition from an online travel agency. Sales manager Richard Deyton has been looking at ways to save costs to avoid damage to the company. He wants to call a meeting of the Sales team to discuss his ideas.

A You are Kim Linford, part of the sales team at Briefcase Travel. Richard has sent everyone an email to arrange a meeting on Tuesday afternoon. Read his email and make notes to prepare for the meeting.

EMAIL

Dear all

As you know, there has been a significant drop in sales this last quarter (see attached statistics). I have been looking at ways to improve the current situation and would like to discuss my ideas with you. Here is a brief outline of my proposal.

We currently employ five full-time members of staff to answer telephone enquiries and advise customers over the phone. The number of online queries is increasing, but the majority of our customers still enquire by phone as they appreciate our personal service. One way to counter the drop in sales and save money is to cut down on staff costs. For example, we could employ an external call centre to do the job instead of having so many full-time staff members. This would not only be much cheaper, but the call centre staff could also additionally promote our services through telemarketing – calling customers and potential customers to inform them of our special offers, etc. In my opinion, this strategy would not only save us money, but could also draw a significant amount of new customers at very little cost.

What do you all think about this idea? Can you think of any additional advantages – or even disadvantages? Any other thoughts?

I suggest meeting at 3 p.m. on Tuesday for about an hour. Please let me know if you can make it.

Thanks and best wishes
Richard

16

B It's Tuesday afternoon and the meeting has just begun. Listen to the conversation and make notes on Carol's and Ranjit's opinions.

C Richard has just asked for your opinion. Write a short answer to his question explaining your views after hearing all the points from the other participants.

D Replace the underlined words with a discussion phrase from the box. There are more discussion phrases than you need.

> can't go along • cutting in • convinced that • hold on a second • is your opinion •
> might be true • should consider • see what I mean • would you agree • you're joking

1 In my opinion, we <u>need to think about</u> getting offers from other international suppliers.
2 Do you <u>understand what I'm trying to say?</u>
3 I am <u>100% certain</u> this is the right decision.
4 I'm sorry, but I <u>really don't agree</u> with you there.
5 <u>Wait a minute</u>, please. I would like to add something important.
6 <u>Seriously?</u> He wanted us to install all his windows for free?
7 Hmm… interesting point. What <u>do you think</u>, Katie?

9 Bilder und Cartoons beschreiben und analysieren

> Bilder und Cartoons beschreiben und analysieren: SB p. 218
> weitere Beispielaufgaben: SB p. 114

SITUATION You have just joined the editorial team of the Pulse online newsletter. The focus of the next issue is "the world of work". You have been asked to choose suitable illustrations for each article.

A Describe and analyse the picture and cartoons. Write at least 100 words about each one.

CAREFUL, YOU'LL UPSET DAD'S WORK/LIFE BALANCE.

"We look for people who can quickly adapt to changes in the workplace."

B Look at the overview of the contents of the newsletter and match the picture and cartoons above to the most suitable article.

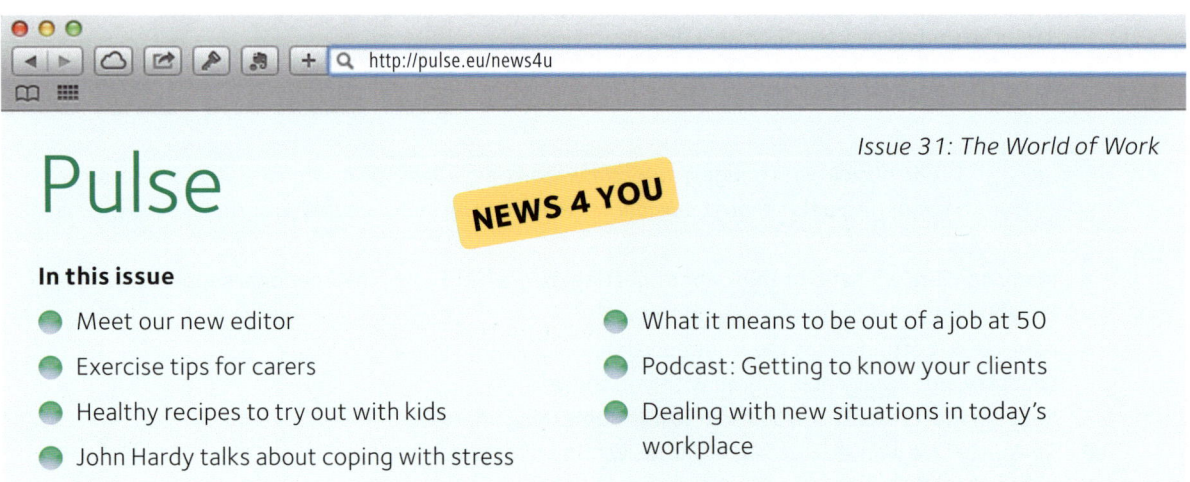

http://pulse.eu/news4u

Issue 31: The World of Work

Pulse

NEWS 4 YOU

In this issue

- Meet our new editor
- Exercise tips for carers
- Healthy recipes to try out with kids
- John Hardy talks about coping with stress
- What it means to be out of a job at 50
- Podcast: Getting to know your clients
- Dealing with new situations in today's workplace

10 Einen Text zusammenfassen

> *Einen Text zusammenfassen: SB p. 216*
> *weitere Beispielaufgaben: SB p. 126*

SITUATION You are shadowing a counsellor who works with the victims of both traditional bullying and cyberbullying. You have found an interesting article describing a case in the United States which you would like to discuss with the counsellor.

A Read the article and summarize the information in about 130 words.

Teenage bullies get off after 12-year-old victim commits suicide

Rebecca S. committed suicide after being repeatedly bullied in person and online.

Two months ago, Rebecca Ann S. committed suicide by jumping from a tower at a disused cement plant. Rebecca was 12 years old.

5 Today, an American court decided to drop charges against two other girls, Katelyn R. (12) and Guadalupe S. (14) who were accused of contributing to Rebecca's death.

At a news conference announcing the arrests of the two girls in October, the judge said that the pair 10 began picking on Rebecca about a year ago after Guadalupe S. started to go out with Rebecca's ex-boyfriend. The older girl threatened Rebecca and said she wanted to fight with her. She also told her to "drink bleach and die". According to the 15 judge, Guadalupe S. persuaded 12-year-old Katelyn to bully Rebecca. The two younger girls had been best friends in the past but they had had no contact since December, when they had a fight which ended their friendship.

20 After Rebecca's death, the older girl was believed to have posted a comment on Facebook in which she admitted bullying her. In this post, she said she didn't care that the 12 year old had killed herself.

During the trial, defence lawyers for the teen-25 agers said that thousands of Facebook messages had been analysed but they did not contain enough evidence to convict the girls. Though the social media messages included things that some children could find upsetting, the defence said that insulting 30 someone and calling them horrible names was not a crime. Katelyn R.'s lawyer said that the posts actually show that she had also been bullied.

After the court's decision had been announced, a counsellor who advises on bullying at schools said the case was difficult right from the start. "Pointing 35 the finger at cyberbullying in a case like Rebecca's is the wrong way to go," she said. "A lot of different things play a part in a suicide."

The counsellor's statement was backed up by a member of the Cyberbullying Research Center. 40 "How can we prove that something posted online can lead to someone taking their own life?", he said. "Most young people who have committed suicide have other elements in their lives that might trigger the action." 45

According to the police, Rebecca was a delicate child who did not have an easy time at home. It appears that she had been cutting herself and was ordered to get psychiatric help last December.

Katelyn's father said, "The court had nothing 50 on the girls. My daughter had a fight with Rebecca a year ago, then they had no more contact. My daughter was expelled from school", he went on, "and the whole family has been threatened and insulted." 55

Katelyn's lawyer asked for an apology from the court for arresting his client and said she was a "troubled young girl" who had been bullied herself.

At a news conference later, the judge said he was happy with the way things turned out. "The two 60 girls involved will get the help they need. My goal was that these kids would never bully anyone again", he said. Katelyn R. and Guadalupe S. will receive counselling.   (514 words)

B Write an email to the counsellor attaching the summary you wrote for exercise A. Give your opinion about the case in the email.

11 Schaubilder und Statistiken beschreiben und analysieren

> *Schaubilder und Statistiken beschreiben und analysieren: SB p. 218*
> *weitere Beispielaufgaben: SB p. 138*

SITUATION Your company wants to make better use of social media. You have joined a workgroup to study and report on long-term social media trends.

A Study the line graph carefully, then choose the correct options to complete the summary below.

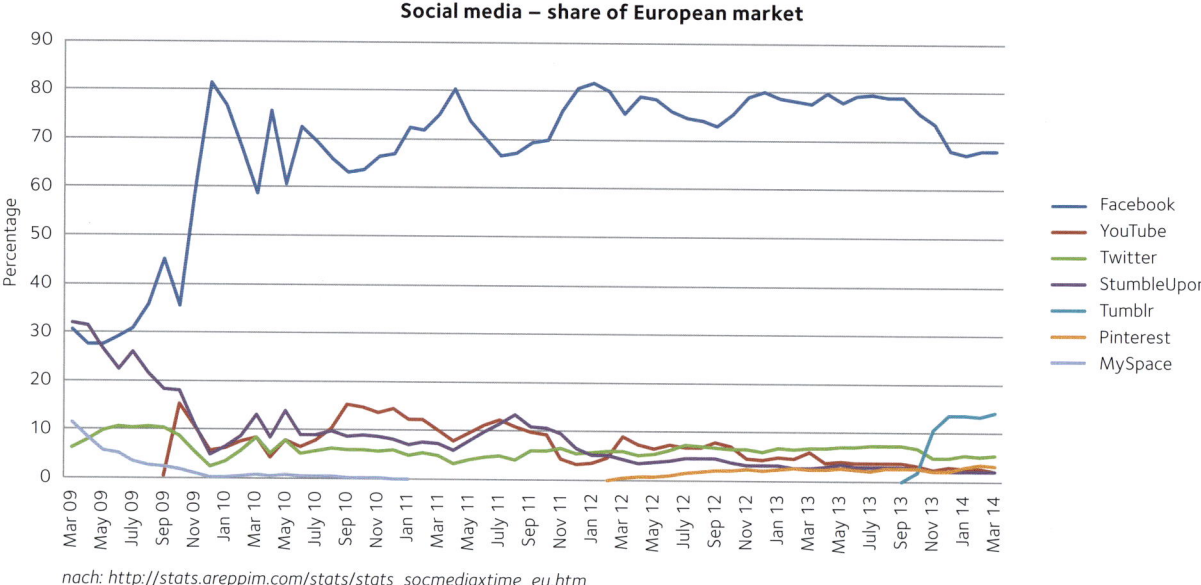

nach: http://stats.areppim.com/stats/stats_socmediaxtime_eu.htm

In March 2009, Facebook's market share was a moderate 30%. It *declined/rose*[1] in June 2009 but then *dropped/jumped*[2] in September to about 45% before *dipping/surging*[3] again and then *plummeting/soaring*[4] to a *peak/all-time low*[5] of just over 80% by December 2009. Since then Facebook's market share has been generally high but has *fluctuated considerably/remained stable*[6] between 60% and 80%. Since September 2013 there are signs of a *downward/upward*[7] trend.

StumbleUpon's market share followed an almost opposite pattern to Facebook's. In March 2009 it had the largest share of the market, at over 30%, but then *slumped/improved*[8] *gradually/sharply*[9] to around 5% and then *fluctuated/stabilized*[10] between around 15% and 5%. Since September 2011 it has shown an overall *downward/upward*[11] trend.

Twitter by contrast has *fluctuated erratically/remained stable*[12] between 5% and 10% for the entire period.

B Describe the market performance of MySpace and Tumblr in the line graph.

C Describe and analyse the bar chart. Write about 150 words.

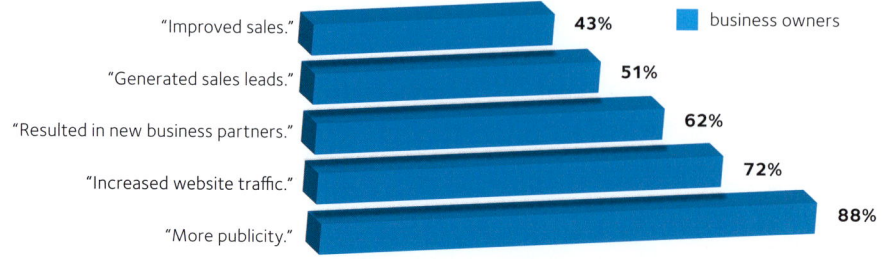

nach: Social Media Marketing Industry Report 2011, www.socialmediaexaminer.com

12 Mediation

❯ *Mediation: SB p. 219*
❯ *weitere Beispielaufgaben: SB p. 150*

SITUATION You are researching the possibility of setting up a 3D printing facility for your school's design and engineering courses.

A Sie finden die folgende Pressemitteilung des 3D-Drucker-Herstellers MakerBot im Internet. Sie fragen sich, ob sich ein MakerBot Innovation Center als gemeinsames Projekt der berufsbildenden Schulen in Ihrer Stadt und der örtlichen Fachhochschule realisieren ließe. Fassen Sie die relevanten Informationen in einer E-Mail an Ihre Schuldirektorin zusammen. Erwähnen Sie darin folgende Punkte:

1. Was ein MakerBot Innovation Center ist
2. Was MakerBot damit bewirken will
3. Vorteile für die Ausbildungsstätte und die Lernenden
4. Wie die Lehranstalt den Zugang zum Innovation Center gestalten könnte

MakerBot Announces Innovation Centers for Universities and Businesses

Brooklyn, N.Y., February 6, 2014 – MakerBot, a global leader in desktop 3D printing, aims at helping transform universities and businesses into MakerBot Innovation Centers that empower organizations to
5 innovate faster, collaborate better and increase their competitity. The MakerBot Innovation Centers are filled with 30+ MakerBot desktop 3D printers and scanners with the goal of helping train the next generation of engineers, architects, industrial
10 designers and artists.

The MakerBot Innovation Center is designed to be a large-scale 3D printing destination, built in partnership with MakerBot and its knowledgeable engineering, creative and training teams. The MakerBot Innovation
15 Centers are intended to increase innovation and collaboration, and work as a catalyst for new ideas and growth. The MakerBot Innovation Centers include a forum to bring departments and individuals together to take education or corporate work to the next level.

By utilizing the MakerBot Innovation Center's 20 numerous MakerBot 3D printers and scanners, the Innovation Center can generate numerous prototypes and models and streamline workflow, as well as being a center for inspiration.

The MakerBot Innovation Centers were conceived 25 to be used by multiple departments in corporations or universities that need access to 3D printing and scanning. At university level, a MakerBot Innovation Center can be open to the student body, and often the community, as a destination to foster innovation. On 30 the business side, MakerBot Innovation Centers can be used as a center for design, product development, rapid prototyping and even small-scale manufacturing.

(239 words)

B Die Schuldirektorin bittet Sie, sich per E-Mail an MakerBot zu wenden, um weitere Details zu erfragen. Verfassen Sie die E-Mail auf Englisch.

Ich habe die Idee mit der Lehrerschaft besprochen und wir finden sie im Prinzip ausgezeichnet. Allerdings hegen wir Zweifel, ob Schulen (und gerade Schulen außerhalb der USA) teilnahmeberechtigt sind.

Würden Sie bitte MakerBot schreiben und um weitere Informationen bitten? Insbesondere brauchen wir folgende Auskünfte:

- Bedingungen für die Teilnahme: Mindestgröße der beteiligten Lehranstalt; ob auch außerhalb der USA; verschiedene Schulformen oder nur Universitäten?
- Ob sich mehrere Lehranstalten zusammenschließen dürfen, um ein solches Zentrum zu betreiben
- Evtl. Verpflichtungen seitens der Lehranstalt: Beteiligung an PR-Aktionen, Werbung; finanzielle Beteiligung; Versicherung der Maschinen
- Unterstützung im Falle von technischen Pannen und Störungen
- Zeitlicher Rahmen: ob befristet oder dauerhaft

QUELLENVERZEICHNIS

Bildrechte

Titelfoto: Shutterstock, nikkytok

Vorwort: S. 2 www.papagei.com; S. 4 Shutterstock, kurhan; S. 7 Shutterstock, arek_malang; S. 8 Youthnet, London; S. 10 / 1 Shutterstock, photoline; / 2 Shutterstock, Nattika; / 3 Shutterstock, Ljyupco; / 4 Shutterstock, Smokovski; / 5 Shutterstock, Oleksiy Mark; / 6 Shutterstock, cristi180884; / 7 Shutterstock, Nattika; / 8 Shutterstock, Kim Nguyen; / 9 Shutterstock, cristi180884; S. 11 Ullstein Bild, AP; S. 12 Shutterstock, kostudio; S. 15 Shutterstock, Jasminko Ibrakovic; S. 17 Shutterstock, baranq; S. 18 Shutterstock, Gil C; S. 19 Videostandbild Scrooser Manufactory, www.scrooser.com; S. 20 / 1 Oxford Designers & Illustrators (ODI); / 2 Shutterstock, bignecker; S. 21 / 1 Oxford Designers & Illustrators (ODI); / 2 Oxford Designers & Illustrators (ODI); / 3 Oxford Designers & Illustrators (ODI); / 4 Oxford Designers & Illustrators (ODI); S. 23 www.papagei.com; S. 24 Shutterstock, Pixel Memoirs; S. 25 / 1 Shutterstock, Hank Frentz; / 2 Shutterstock, Ermolaev Alexander; S. 26 Fotolia, hartphotography; S. 29 Shutterstock, CREATISTA; S. 33 / 1 Shutterstock, Jianhao Guan; / 2 cartoonstock, Jon Carter; S. 34 Oxford Designers & Illustrators (ODI); S. 35 / 1 Shutterstock, Francis L Fruit; / 2 Shutterstock, BlueSkyImage; S. 36 mauritius images, Cultura; S. 39 / 1 Shutterstock, J. McPhail; / 2 Shutterstock, Kyle Lee; S. 41 Shutterstock, Monkey Business Images; S. 43 Shutterstock, wavebreakmedia; S. 44 Shutterstock, Hasloo Group Production Studio; S. 45 Shutterstock, g-stockstudio; S. 49 Shutterstock, D. Hammonds; S. 50 Shutterstock, Peter Bernik; S. 51 / 1 Shutterstock, pashabo; / 2 Shutterstock, Robert Hillmann; S. 53 Shutterstock, erichon; S. 54 Shutterstock, hxdbbzxy; S. 55 Shutterstock, Pressmaster; S. 57 cartoonstock, Bill Proud; S. 59 Shutterstock, Pal Teravagimov; S. 60 Shutterstock, Fenton one; S. 61 Videostandbild www.papagei.com; S. 63 Dave Hakken; S. 65 Shutterstock, Pressmaster; S. 66 Shutterstock, Stocklite; S. 68 Shutterstock, Gyuszko-Photo; S. 69 / 1 cartoonstock, Mark Lynch; / 2 www.solarimpulse.com; S. 70 www.google.com/glass; S. 72 Shutterstock, wavebreakmedia; S. 73 / 1 Shutterstock, StockLite; / 2 Shutterstock, AVAVA; / 3 Shutterstock, MUTH; S. 74 Videostandbild www.papagei.com; S. 77 Shutterstock, Evdokimov Maxim; S. 82 / 1 Shutterstock, Robert Kneschke; / 2 European Commission, Directorate General for Education and Culture, Youth Unit, Brussels; S. 83 Fotolia, Monkey Business; S. 84 / 1 mauritius images, Tetra Images; / 2 Cartoonsy, Flanagan; / 3 cartoonstock.com, Mike Baldwin

Videorechte

Video 1, S. 8: "Job interview body language", www.youthnet.org
Video 2, S. 19: "Scrooser Kickstarter Promo", Scrooser Manufactory, www. scrooser.com
Video 3, S. 23: "Just a Family", NY Times,
https://www.nytimes.com/video/us/100000001090280/just-a-family.html
Video 4, S. 61: "Human Impact: Pacific plastic Hawaii", BBC Earth
https://www.youtube.com/watch?v=9eefyztmall
Video 5, S. 74: "Drones for hire", NY Times,
https://www.nytimes.com/video/technology/100000001364648/drones-for-hire.html
Video 6, S. 82: "Youth in Action - EVS for refugees", European Commission, Directorate General for Education and Culture, Youth Unit, Brussels

Textrechte

S. 15 / 1 „Magazines 'harm male body image'". Aus: http://news.bbc.co.uk/go/pr/fr/-/2/hi/health/7318411.stm – BBC News, 28.03.2008, / 2 Benjamin O'Keefe's online petition to Abercrombie and Fitch. Aus: http://www.change.org/petitions/abercrombie-fitch-ceo-mike-jeffries-stop-telling-teens-they-aren-t-beautiful-make-clothes-for-teens-of-all-sizes; S. 63 Dave Hakkens, „Precious Plastic Factory". Aus: http://www.dezeen.com/2013/11/11/dave-hakkensprecious-plastic-recycling-machines-movie/; S. 68 John Vidal, „UK and Germany break solar power records". Aus: http://www.theguardian.com/environment/2014/jun/23/uk-and-germany-break-solar-power-records - The Guardian, 23.06.2014; S. 77 Mattia Rosini, „Immigration to Germany at its highest rate". Aus: http://www.west-info.eu/immigration-to-germany-at-its-highest-rate/ – West / Welfare Society Territory, 22.05.2014; S. 78 „Economic refugees choose Germany". Aus: http://rt.com/news/161484-germany-immigration-increase-europe/ – RT News, 26.05.2014; S. 79 Kathy Gyngell, „Legalizing drugs would bring not freedom but enslavement". Aus: http://www.theguardian.com/commentisfree/2014/feb/20/legalising-drugs-pro-drug-liberals-sideeffects-children-experiment – The Guardian, 20.02.2014; S. 87 „MakerBot Announces Innovation Centers for Universities and Business". Pressemitteilung (Auszug) aus: http://makerbot-blog.s3.amazonaws.com/wpcontent/uploads/2014/02/Rls_InnovationCenter_Feb2014_f.pdf

Audiorechte

© Cornelsen Schulverlage GmbH, Berlin; Produktion: Clarity Studio, Berlin